six
funerals
and a
wedding

six
funerals
and a
wedding

a memoir

Mary Twomey Odgers

with Stacey Aaronson

KINGS PARK

Kings Park Press
kingsparkpress@gmail.com

ISBN: 978-1-7340939-0-2 pbk
ISBN: 978-1-7340939-1-9 hc
ISBN: 978-1-7340939-2-6 ebk

Library of Congress Control Number: 2020902397

Book design by Stacey Aaronson

Printed in the United States of America

To David and Matthew
You, my sons, are
the beat of my heart,
the best of my life

To Pierre
My silver lining
My hope for tomorrow

To John
Loss bound us together
Love guided our way

introduction

*O*F ALL THE EMOTIONS HUMANS EXPERIENCE, THE one with the greatest number of manifestations has to be grief. I know this to be true because in a span of eight weeks, I lost my husband, my father, and my youngest son, all in traumatic ways, and all of which came on the heels of losing our home and everything in it to a wildfire just one year prior.

Nothing could have prepared me for any of those losses, and I didn't experience a single one of them in the same way. I felt like a plastic bag on the highway, dipping and crashing into oncoming traffic, then being whipped into the air again, having no idea where I might land.

During the ensuing years, some of the most joyful pockets of time for me were those when I would meet someone new who didn't yet know my tragic backstory, which meant that for a brief period of time, I wasn't defined by the soul-piercing losses everyone in my circle had learned to dance around in their own way. I was just Mary. A registered nurse. Mother of two grown sons. Single. Not the woman people whispered about or felt sorry for. Because the truth is, few of us know how to operate in the presence of someone who has suffered great loss. Do you say something and risk upsetting them? Or do you say nothing and risk seeming unfeeling? Do you offer to merely hold them with no words spoken? Or would that kind of affection feel too invasive, too inappropriate?

I can tell you that at times, all of those felt awkward or unwelcome, or comforting and appreciated, depending on my state of mind that day. This is in part why I say the most nuanced of human emotions is grief. I felt every extreme, every lift and sway and descent that a person can feel. And yet, only a few years later, when I lost my brother and shortly afterward my mother, I wasn't "seasoned" in the arena of grief. Personally, I don't believe a person can be. Because every loss is unique, every relationship to what's been lost different. This is what I've endeavored to portray in sharing with you an intimate vignette of each entity and person I've had to say goodbye to. Whether it's a loved one, a friend, a marriage, a home; the loss of a job or a child going off to college; or even the loss of yourself as you once knew, you must embark on a process of letting go and facing a new reality.

This is not a prescriptive book on the topics of grief or reinvention; myriad books exist that attempt to walk someone through the stages of mourning or that offer guidance for navigating life-altering change and starting anew. Rather, this is my story—a story of family, with all its joys and bumps, proud moments and regrets. And yes, one of profound loss, but also of profound growth—one I wrote not only for myself and my sons, but also because I know there are numerous people who have faced circumstances that took more from them than seemed humanly possible. Whether or not you are one of those people, I wrote this book to encourage you, to tell you that it is possible to survive devastation beyond measure, to find happiness when your heart is broken beyond recognition, to pursue a new direction when your life plan has been derailed, and to even find love again when it might seem impossible.

Your path will always be your own, but my prayer is that this book will inspire you to see the world in a broader context of love, as well as in tiny pockets of divine gifts, even when you feel as if you're constantly dodging shards of sadness, struggling to find your way when your world has been upended.

I want you to know that I've been there.

I also want you to know that, together with my sons—sometimes trudging uphill a few feet only to slide further than I had climbed—I gathered the strength to pull myself higher until I gradually, miraculously, found my way.

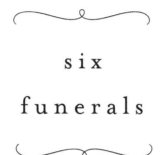

six

funerals

house

I SAT AT MY DESK AND NEARLY FELT THE POWER of the wind move through me as I watched it blow the pepper and citrus trees on the upward slope of our yard. A long, gray stream of smoke billowed beyond the hills that bordered our house, but fires were common this time of year, so I didn't give it much thought. Besides, the howling Santa Anas were carrying the fire in the opposite direction on that October day in 2007.

It had been eighteen years since my husband Bruce and I found the 9.3 acres overlooking the Santa Maria Valley and majestic Mount Woodson in Ramona, California. With its sweeping views, varied topography, and stunning sunsets, we determined it was the perfect place to build our dream house. After living for nearly a decade in Texas, where Bruce was a Delta Airlines pilot and we'd been raising our three little boys, I was more than eager to return to Southern California. So, eagerly on my part, a bit reluctantly on Bruce's, we purchased the property with retirement money, a huge dose of hope, and a lot of prayers.

The suburban Plano, Texas, market where we lived was flat and had been for years; one of the nicer houses on our street had sat on the market for two years. Within a few months, the strain of our house payment and the California land payment was upon us, and though we had no reason to expect our luck would be any different than our neighbors', we put the Plano house on the market. Miraculously, it sold in one month to a couple who had looked at it the first day. Moving to California to build our dream house was no longer something we only fantasized about—it was about to become our reality.

By August 1989, our three little "helpers"—David was seven, Matthew was four, and baby Patrick was a year and a half—had done their part to assist my brother Michael and me in carefully packing dozens of boxes in preparation for our three-state leap. Michael lived in Texas, too, and had been devoted to us during our years there. Every Sunday, he drove over and spent the day with us, endearing himself to the boys as their favorite uncle. He had traversed some tough times with addiction and found a haven in our home full of happy activity. His great sense of humor proved just what we needed during the stress of packing—in a burst of creativity, he suggested we come up with humorous labels to write on the boxes with our big black markers, such as: "objects d'art," "scary stuff from boys rooms," "icky treasures from master bath," and "Julia Child's Wannabe Spot." No doubt, Michael made the arduous task of moving a lot more fun, but he was also one of the biggest reasons it made leaving achingly difficult.

AFTER WE SETTLED into our temporary California home and began our plans to build, it didn't take long to discover that we had invested in acreage that came with myriad challenges. First, we weren't located in the Ramona water district, so we had to go to the great expense of drilling a well into the dense granite earth. Second, with no power source on the property, we had to find a way to harness it from surrounding resources.

Third, the natural landscape was lovely but dry, and intermittent winds stirred up floating allergens of every kind. And the dips and swells that were byproducts of the land weren't the only tests.

Not long after the move, Bruce's introspective moods became frequent and perplexing visitors. Though he had wanted to move back to California too, I was the one who had pushed it, striving to dull his constant worry with my ray of optimism. But nothing I did or said seemed to reach him.

During the construction, Bruce—who preferred control without having to appease me—seldom solicited my opinions. He was completely capable in the building of the house, but he also became an expert at erecting walls between us. He wasn't deliberately trying to shut me out; he was simply wired in a way that made him more of a tough shell I couldn't penetrate than a willfully unfeeling spouse. And because of that wiring, the more I complained or became impatient, the more he resisted me—which caused us both to foster resentment toward each other. When I felt strongly about something and spoke up about it, my suggestion was often met with defensiveness, along with an unconvincing excuse why it wasn't possible. For example, I'd always dreamed of having a fireplace in the kitchen, one that also faced the living room. Because we could build our home however we wanted to, it seemed like a perfectly reasonable wish.

"We can't afford it," he would quietly, but with conviction, say each time I brought it up.

Defaulting to the complacent wife role wasn't at all where I felt comfortable, but I grew tired of trying to convince him it would all work out. So even though I didn't feel like a huge player in the process of planning our family home, instead of becoming defensive, I fell back on the adaptive personality trait fostered in me from a very young age and resigned myself to being lucky to build a dream house at all. As it was, the stages of development were often so drawn out that even the most patient person would be challenged to tolerate them. That, coupled with Bruce's inability to incorporate the majority of my ideas, sucked all the fun out of what should have been a joyful partnership project.

Perhaps I should have seen it as an omen of sorts.

AFTER WE OFFICIALLY moved in on March 10, 1992, our 10,000-gallon tank loomed on the highest part of our land, feeding our home and the surrounding chaparral, buckwheat, and sumac with gravity-produced water. Electricity had been magically—albeit painstakingly—brought to our land, lighting our house on the hill like a beacon of sorts. And our living room fireplace crackled with eucalyptus logs we hauled in from outside. (We were supposed to have natural gas, but it somehow never made it onto the blueprint.) This rustic addition to our country-style existence was quaint, but I admit I didn't relish walking beyond the large, circular concrete driveway at night to collect firewood piled at the edge of the citrus grove. I would kick myself for forgetting to retrieve wood during daylight hours; nights were always pitch black and coyotes howled in the distance. Any type of wildlife could have rushed me at any moment, and I knew the logs could be fraught with spiders and God only knows what else. So while I didn't love the task of retrieving the wood itself, witnessing the atmosphere it brought to evenings with our family of five always made it worth the trek.

By our first summer's end, we were perhaps introduced to the most disconcerting part of living in our gorgeous hamlet:

the fierce and unpredictable Santa Ana winds. When they swept through, they were enough to make a person wish they were anywhere but overlooking that grand, beautiful valley. They screamed through the hills from the desert to the coast, making it scorching in the fall and freezing in the winter, drying us and everything else alive into a parched state. Their wailing kept us awake at night as they uprooted anything we prized outdoors and blew it to oblivion. Not even an iron trampoline could hold its ground; once the winds stopped, often as suddenly as they arrived, we would have to gather the trampoline piece by heavy piece and reassemble it all over again. And there was more not to love: the well once went dry, the winter rains eroded the landscaping, the rabbits made growing grass nearly impossible, and the owls and coyotes took many of our beloved cats and one precious dog named Benji.

But despite all that, something spoke to my heart about that land. When the weather and wild animals weren't wreaking havoc, it was impossible not to be enveloped in the fragrance of the biannual blossoms of the orange, grapefruit, and tangerine trees we planted; in the peaceful sound of nighttime silence punctuated only by the occasional chatter of a coyote or owl; in the pitch blackness of night that made the blanket of stars look like a treasure chest. I'd heard people say they felt small in comparison to the celestial canopy over my head, but it never made me feel that way. Instead, I felt ethereal and wondered, *How could I be so lucky?* Yes, despite the concrete disadvantages of living in an environment where the energy was undoubtedly volatile, of all the places I could have raised our children, Ramona endlessly spoke to that special place in my heart that could never ignore all the remarkable parts of creation that surrounded me as blessings.

But three years after settling into the long-awaited embrace of our house and its particular rustic endearments, I was still not able to shake what I can only describe as a persistent sense of restlessness, as if I were a stranger in my own home. I couldn't pinpoint where it stemmed from, but it was almost palpable—only I knew I would be hard-pressed to make anyone, especially Bruce, understand it.

One evening, after the boys were in bed, I joined Bruce on the couch as he flipped through channels on the remote.

"Something must be wrong with me," I said with a sigh. "I find it hard to feel at home here in this house."

He turned to me slowly. In his always deliberate manner, he said, "What do you mean? I thought you wanted this?"

What I wanted to say was:

If we're honest about it, building a home was something YOU always wanted. Don't get me wrong, I loved the idea and am in awe of you making something like this happen, but I'm having trouble really settling into this house like I thought I would.

Instead, I simply said:

"I guess it is. I don't know . . . like I said, something must be wrong with me."

Bruce simply shrugged in agreement, leaving me feeling even more alienated about my feelings than before.

SHORTLY AFTER OUR awkward exchange, I attended a Feng Shui presentation, where I learned all about the art of creating harmonious surroundings that enhance the yin and yang—male and female—energy, and how spatial arrangement changes the energetic flow, which creates a more favorable sense of happiness and relaxation in one's space. The presenter was available for consultations, so I took the opportunity to schedule one with her, filled with hope that the ancient Chinese practice might make a difference for me. When I mentioned it to Bruce, he surprised me.

"Whatever makes you happy," he said. "I'm game if you are."

While Bruce may have been a master at shutting me out, he also never deliberately wanted to leave me feeling hurt or unheard. I know this sounds like a huge contradiction, and it was, but it was simply the way Bruce operated in his world. As with every project he took on, he saw it from only one perspective: his. But once that vision was attained for him, he became open to "making it right" for my sake—which was exactly what happened with our house. After it was complete and his big job was done, he was then willing to entertain an idea of mine that might make me feel happier within the walls he had built. In this case, not only did a rare expression of enthusiasm cross Bruce's face, I also saw a surprising look of relief. I knew that Feng Shui was a foreign concept to him, but it had offered him a reason for why I'd felt so shut out, which seemed to absolve him of having to figure out a mystery he probably felt was impossible to solve. Simply knowing he supported my exploration of the Asian custom reignited a spark of hope in me.

The consultant and I had a brief conversation over the phone before our appointment in which she asked when Bruce's and my birthdays were. I gave her the dates and she jotted them down. Then we planned to meet at our home one day that same week.

From the moment she arrived and stepped foot inside the house, she was full of enthusiastic compliments. The way she chattered on, I expected her to come right out and say I was spoiled. Instead, she wasted no time getting down to business, expressing a welcome understanding of my dilemma.

"Your birth dates," she explained, "show your needs with regard to direction and the energy that has on each individual. You and your husband, I'm afraid, have quite opposite needs."

"Oh," I said, intrigued.

"This doesn't mean you're doomed or anything," she said with a laugh. "You *can* find your way to each other with some changes."

I smiled. "Well, that's good to hear."

"The thing is," she continued, changing her tone to a slightly saddened one, "this house reflects nothing at all of you. It totally speaks to the needs of your husband."

I felt my shoulders fall. I wasn't surprised, but hearing her say the words, I didn't know if I wanted to cry or scream.

"Don't worry, though," she assured me. "We don't need to make any structural changes. We're going to just move a few things, add a few things, and make this the home of your dreams!"

My face burst into a delighted smile, which seemed to be the only response she needed to start the process. She popped up from the couch and proceeded to lead me on a tour of my own house. I grabbed a pad and took copious notes, overwhelmed with happiness that I would finally be making our home mine as well as Bruce's and the boys'.

That evening, I enthusiastically shared with Bruce the meeting I'd had and some of the changes I was eager to make. The earlier relief and interest he had shown returned, and I intuited within our conversation a sense of the powerlessness Bruce had felt in needing to be in charge to the point of excluding me. It seemed contradictory; I always thought that being in charge gave him a sense of *power*, not *powerlessness*. However, I didn't want to rock the boat by trying to make sense of it; I simply wanted to revel in the joy of having found my way to the contentment I lacked—and to do so with what appeared to be Bruce's blessing.

I couldn't have known that those changes, which finally made our house feel like our forever home to me, would be temporary—and not because Bruce ultimately objected to them, but because the Santa Anas on that October day in 2007 suddenly took an unexpected turn.

MATT WAS IN his bedroom, organizing the space he'd always shared with Patrick, who had recently left for Purdue University. The phone had rung several times, and each time Matthew had picked up and chatted with friends and neighbors about the same concern: what their plans were if they had to evacuate.

We had lived with that possibility—and sometimes reality— for the past eighteen years. The brown, scraggly chaparral that covered the terrain and wedged itself between the massive grayish-white and brown granite boulders as far as the eye could see depended on fire to reseed. Funny how the agent neglected to mention that when Bruce and I bought the property. We were far too steeped in the excitement of envisioning our future home to think about things like indigenous plants and seeds and seasonal winds off the desert, so it's no surprise that we never thought to ask if fires might be a concern.

I heard Matt hang up the phone and resume banging around in his room. Shortly after, it rang again, but this time I picked it up.

"Mary? I need your help," a woman's voice said frantically. "I completely forgot about the deadline to have all those t-shirts of the boys' sewn into a memory blanket."

I squeezed my eyes shut and let out a sigh. I had searched the house once or twice and come up with several shirts, including a Bulldogs jersey and tees from RHS Cross Country, Drama, Tennis, Purdue, and the Marine Corps Marathon, but I wanted a representation of the boys' early years. Only I'd completely forgotten about the deadline too. "Yes, okay. I'll get them together and get them over to you," I assured her, surprised she hadn't mentioned the possible threat of the fire.

She hung up relieved, and I made my way to the hall closet where I remembered I'd long ago stashed three plastic bins. As I took each one down and opened it, a flood of memories cascaded over me. Greeting me were numerous items from my sons' infanthood: little white high-top shoes; the stuffed Peter Rabbit that moved his head while playing "Here Comes Peter Cottontail"; the tiniest jeans accompanied by even tinier Nike tennis shoes. I held each item carefully as if I was afraid they would disappear. The comfort I felt, with a little sadness mixed in, represented the beautiful memories of my babies. I knelt down and put my face into the box, hoping—however foolishly—for a fragrance, or simply a small reminder of those times. But that feeling was quickly eclipsed when I found what I was looking for: in multicolored shiny, somewhat cracked, puff paint, the tiny t-shirt read, "The First Annual Cousins Thanksgiving Day Run – 1988." I couldn't believe it was still readable as I put the aging gem in the bag on top of the other shirts, then called for Matt to drive them to the seamstress.

About twenty minutes after he left, he called to tell me that he couldn't find the house and was coming back home.

"What? No, Matt," I said. "You *have* to find the house. She needs the shirts *today.*"

"Geez, Mom . . . okay." I could tell Matt was shocked by my reaction, and frankly, so was I. Normally, I would have been more laid back about it and maybe even let it go. But something propelled a sense of urgency in me. I also knew the seamstress was stressed out, and I didn't want to be the cause of further angst. I gave him directions with better detail, and not long after, he called again to say he'd found the place. At the moment, I was simply relieved. Every square of the blanket would be a segment of a t-shirt from the activities of three growing boys over the years. I looked so forward to being able to hold it in my hands once it was finished.

BY EVENING, the wildfire still raged in the distance, sending plumes of smoke into the air beyond the valley and making our surroundings at once chaotic and quietly eerie. But we had still received no word to evacuate, so as was typical in these pockets of concern we experienced watching the orange-hued sky, I fielded calls and extended invitations to those who were affected to take refuge with our family. I made pizzas I could easily reheat, and I baked my mom's caramel walnut bars as treats. As long as the winds were on our side, and all reports continued to show the gales taking the embers east of us, I expected to welcome friends and provide a place to sleep for everyone, as I had during the big 2003 fire. But at the moment, it was only Matt and I. Bruce was flying and would be home from his layover in Arizona by morning; David was staying in Culver City; and Patrick, typical Patrick, was glued to the news—receiving more information, it seemed, than we were—calling multiple times throughout the day from Purdue to see if we were okay.

After night fell, Matt and I went outside to survey what Mother Nature had brought down on the neighboring area. Embers marched in a straight horizontal line down the tallest distant hills—but the direction was no longer the same as it had been earlier.

"Mom," Matt said. "It looks like the fire's shifted north-west, toward us."

Noticing neighbors leaving up the hill, I felt my heart leap and knew he was right. Scrambling to action as we had numerous times before, we began loading laundry baskets, the easiest method we'd found to transport what we chose to take with us. Matt, ever thoughtful, called his dad and brothers to get their lists of favored items. When Matt saw me moving on the slow side, he urged me to hurry up. But I'd been here before, loading carefully, only to unload tomorrow. I had little doubt that would be the scenario once again—the fires were under control, and by morning, we would likely be safe to return home again.

As I searched out the treasured possessions I wanted to take, just in case our fears indeed materialized, I picked up my Lladro statue of a young mother with a child on her hip. It had been a gift from Bruce and the boys on the Mother's Day just after Patrick was born. That silky smooth piece of porcelain was a perfect representation of what my passion in life was. I carefully wrapped it, concerned about it getting broken from being packed and then unpacked so soon afterward. Even though in my heart I believed I'd be coming back tomorrow, somehow I couldn't leave that statue. So I placed it in the basket with the photo albums, all labeled by year. On my way out, I took one last look around and saw my well-worn recipe book sitting on the counter. It wasn't normally there, and I never would have thought of it with so much on my mind had it not been in plain sight. Each card was handwritten in the unique style of the donors, and it represented years of having people in my home, sharing good company. Grateful that this beloved piece of history caught my eye, I grabbed it and added it to the basket.

Within half an hour of deciding to evacuate, around 11:30 p.m., sixty-mph gales were tearing through our neighborhood at a deafening level. When I opened the door, I was immediately shoved backward. Smoke flooded my lungs and stung my eyes. I bent over my basket as if fighting violent arms and screams of a nature that was angry with humanity and trudged headfirst toward the car. When I yanked on the handle, the heavy door swung fiercely out of my hand and I heard the hinges crack. Shoving the basket in, I steadied myself against the frame to arrange a blanket in the backseat for our dog, Harley. He was terribly arthritic, and lifting him would cause him a lot of pain; being part pit bull, our fear was that he would viciously bite at seeing us attempt to cradle him. Matt quickly grabbed a blanket from his car and fought the gusts to secure it over Harley's head. Knowing how precious little time was left, I lifted Harley in my arms and gently laid him on the seat, forcing the back door shut as the wind battled against me.

"Follow me," I yelled to Matt, pulling the driver door closed with both hands, then swiping the hair from my face the wind had plastered to it.

I heeded my instinct to lead the way out, though following Matt would have allowed me to keep my eyes on him. A wave of smoke could have easily obscured his vision and separated him from me, so I kept watch on his headlights and made sure he was close, forging ahead cloaked in prayer as my heart pounded louder in my ears than the Santa Anas outside.

I don't know if Matt looked back. I can't specifically remember if I did either. All I know is that on some level, consciously or unconsciously, as we drove away under the glow of that raging wildfire just shy of midnight, we said our goodbyes to a home—and a life—that would never be the same again.

WE DROVE DOWN the hill to my best friend Maripat's house, not far from ours but out of the danger zone. Braving the wind, Matt, Harley, and I, along with our friend Susan who had followed us there, made our way inside. I collapsed on the living room couch as a biting cold enveloped me.

"Try to get some rest," Maripat implored, then disappeared to settle the others in various rooms.

I lay there restless for nearly an hour, haunted by the wind knocking brutally on the windows. Suddenly, a loud rap on the front door competed with the gusts outside. Startled, I rushed to the door to find an officer on the porch.

"I'm sorry, ma'am," he said. "You need to evacuate right away." He explained how the fire had turned and that we had little time to leave.

"Is there any word on Ramona?" I asked.

He brought his hands to his belt and clutched it. "Everything on Highland Valley Road has burned."

I let out a little gasp. "We're a mile off Highland Valley."

"Like I said, ma'am, everything's burned on that road."

"But do you think our house . . . being so close?" I looked at him with pleading eyes.

He sighed and nodded slightly as his face softened. "More than likely."

I reasoned that he didn't know for sure. He only knew about Highland Valley Road, not *our* road specifically. Our house couldn't be in danger. It just couldn't be.

In a flurry, we mobilized to help Maripat, who hadn't anticipated evacuating and had nothing packed. We grabbed jewelry, photos, a few keepsakes, and within fifteen minutes, we had begun our caravan toward the coast.

With so many people fleeing the upper neighborhoods, it took a few stops before we found a hotel with a single room available—and even then, we had to wait for it to be cleaned. By that point, it was nearing dawn, so we took refuge in the restaurant where we kept vigil until the sun's misty rays brightened the smoky-gray sky.

As I sipped on yet another cup of coffee, I thought about our phone message service, a satellite that was attached to our roof rather than a remote AT&T station. Something propelled me to call, so I excused myself from the group and found a quiet corner. As the phone rang and rang, I remembered Bruce saying that if the Santa Anas ever knocked the satellite down, we wouldn't get any phone messages. With the gusts we had driven away in, I knew that was likely. But when no voice recording clicked on, my intuition told me that it wasn't just the wind.

I rejoined our table without saying a word, shoving my suspicions into a proverbial vault. When a friend from Oklahoma called, I said we still knew nothing.

Once we were allowed into our hotel room, I was able to contact our neighbor from across the street, a woman we didn't know well but who I suspected hadn't evacuated with the rest of us.

"Mary . . . yes," she said. "I know who you are."

"Oh good." I took a breath. "Did you decide to stay? Do you know how the neighborhood is?"

"We did," she said. "There was no way we were going to leave our horses." She paused. "And yes . . . there was a lot of damage here."

I gasped. "Do you happen to know if our house is still standing?"

She was silent for only a moment. "Your house, Mary . . . it's gone."

I felt a numbness move through my body. "Are you sure?"

"Yes, I'm sure."

"Our house is the one that has the line of palm trees backing the pool . . . you know, directly across from yours."

"Yes, I know," she said.

Grasping for any evidence that she'd made a mistake, I bit my lip and searched for another feature she could reference. "It has the 10,000-gallon tank sitting up above."

"Yes," she confirmed again, patient but firm. "It's your house, Mary."

I shook my head. "Gone? Is it a complete burn or just part of it?"

She took an audible breath. "It's the whole thing," she said with compassion. "I'm so sorry."

Surrendering to what I already knew but was desperately trying to deny, I swallowed hard and thanked her, then hung up in a daze, unable to move.

Seemingly within seconds, my phone rang again. It was our neighbor, Jeff. He could often be a gruff New Yorker, but that morning he was gentle and kind as he patiently helped the reality sink in.

"I just got off the phone with Bruce," he told me. "He's on his way to the hotel." He paused and lowered his voice slightly. "He already knows."

I felt my heart sink with both relief and anxiety. "Oh . . . okay. That's good, I guess."

"Probably," he agreed.

But the truth was, I didn't know what to feel.

He wished me well, saying we'd talk again soon. I nodded and flipped my phone closed. Several pairs of eyes were on me, but I only remember the faces of three: Matt, Maripat, and her husband Ken.

"We lost it," I said.

Mouths dropped, eyes shifted. No one said a word. Everyone seemed to sink into a palpable state of disbelief.

Only moments later, the door opened with a loud click. It was Bruce. I immediately went to him and we embraced. But even under those circumstances, when a couple would naturally cling to each other, I could feel that he was preoccupied with the world on his shoulders, that his arms around me were more perfunctory than heartfelt.

He released me quickly and started making phone calls, each in his calm, business-like manner. Last, he called his parents. He had kept his emotions in check until then, but when he spoke to his mother, I heard his voice falter. When I looked over at him, I saw his eyes welling with tears.

In that moment, I wanted to cry with him over our loss, but I realized it wasn't the time for that. Something inside him went into autopilot, and that state didn't include me. Though I had a brief sensation of sadness over it, I didn't begrudge him for it. I knew it was simply his way of coping. So, despite the decimating nature of what we were going through, I turned to my friends and my son for shared strength—and silently to God for his help in getting us through it.

THAT NIGHT IN the hotel room, with Matt on the rollaway twin bed and Maripat and Ken in the queen bed across from us, Bruce and I held each other tightly in the dark. As I took refuge in his arms, in that sacred pocket of time I'll always treasure, I whispered to him how much I appreciated his making certain we were insured and taken care of for an event like this. I couldn't see his face, but I like to imagine that in the midst of our lives being stripped to the bare minimum, with nothing but my words of gratitude to buoy the immeasurable heaviness I know he felt, he allowed himself a moment of serenity—one he would sadly never find again in the months to come.

IN THE DAYS immediately following, David and Patrick came home. We obtained a FEMA number—which allowed us to partake in the shelters and supply stations they set up for the victims—and opened a claim with our insurance company. We had no clothes except what we were wearing, so we made a trip to Costco to get some things. There, in that warehouse filled to the hilt with tables upon tables of clothing and rows and boxes of undergarments and shoes, I felt an inexplicable sense of invasion creep into me that those new items represented. Perhaps it was that I couldn't make any decisions just then, whether big or small, or maybe I simply couldn't bear anything new trying to replace what I'd just lost, but a pair of jeans was all I could bring myself to choose in the moment. Thank God for Maripat, who was an endless source of encouragement during that time, or I might have gone through life like a zombie for a week.

WITHIN TWO DAYS, the authorities deemed it safe to return to our property. As the five of us wound up the road toward our lot, evidence that the fire had run like a river through our neighborhood was a startling sight. Fences were burned or melted, depending on the material, as if the inferno had chosen its doors to open and move through. Some people had lost only a storage shed or stable, similar to the aftermath of a tornado, as the flaming path bypassed their houses, while others had lost everything. Each of us lived on eight-plus acre lots, so seeing so many empty—or near-empty—plots of land made the area feel almost apocalyptic.

Turning slowly onto our street, we all searched for the six palm trees up on the right, the Canary palms that sheltered the path from the driveway, the pepper trees that greeted us once at the end of the circle drive. But all that remained were ashes. Very little of our land was recognizable; it actually felt as though the decimated grounds emitted echoes that our house had been a primary target.

"Oh my God," I muttered as Bruce came to a stop.

Matthew looked at me in silence as I brought my hand to my mouth. After several seconds of stillness, we gently opened the doors and got out. Each of us looked down at the strange feeling of our shoes sinking into ash. Then we gazed out into the vastness of the now desolate space, with the exception of only a few remains—and the horror of our neighbors walking through our rubble.

With barely ten seconds to catch our breath and take in the enormity of our loss, the couple turned to greet us. "Hi guys . . . we're *so* sorry. This is just awful."

We were speechless. We would have only this one opportunity to see what was left of our home, and this couple, while well-intentioned, didn't realize they were trespassing on our hearts. What should have been a sacred family moment of emotional release or bonding with each other was shattered. While we were cordial, we couldn't help but wonder why they didn't stay back and observe from a distance, giving us our space. And just when we thought it couldn't get any more awkward or uncomfortable, another neighbor whose house was still standing ambled up the driveway. I assumed that she, too, had come to comfort us, only to be taken aback when she handed me her husband's drywalling business card.

"He'll give you a really good price," she promised.

It was all I could do to force a smile that was anything but sincere.

I don't recall how long the neighbors lingered, only that it was far too long for anyone's comfort. Encircled by the acrid air—both literally and figuratively—it took everything in me to remain polite. When they finally took their overdue leave, the relief I felt was paradoxical: When does anyone wish someone would hurry up and leave so they can get to the gut-wrenching business of viewing the seared remains of their life? It was like a play in three increasingly unsettling acts: shock, intrusion, devastation.

We quietly began stumbling through the wreckage, each in our own stupefied state. Patrick, who we called "The Finder" because he always seemed to find everything that had gone missing, surveyed the land then headed out as if on a mission, walking straight to where Bruce's office had been.

"Check this out," he called, holding up the burned remains of a handgun we'd kept locked in a closet.

"Oh, wow," I heard Matthew say, the ground crunching under his shoes as he moved closer to see it. But my eyes had fallen on something else: a black wall amidst the grayish-black ashes that didn't make sense to me. I approached it carefully as we'd been shown to do so we wouldn't fall or step on something that could injure us. Once I reached the wall, I ran my fingertips over the ebony façade. Underneath the ash was the white Japanese porcelain tile we had so thoughtfully chosen years before for our master bathroom. Seeing it there, like a lone standing symbol of what was no longer, flooded my consciousness with proof of how our lives had changed forever.

Standing in that space, I flashed on the phone call I had with my mother the day before. She and my dad had been their usual encouraging selves; they remarked how much they had loved all the times they'd spent in our country home, lamenting that there would be no more but striving to focus on the positive. And then the question I hoped my mother wouldn't ask came tumbling out.

"Did you get the album?"

I swallowed hard. I had just celebrated my fiftieth birthday, and my mother had lovingly crafted a beautiful scrapbook of memorabilia and photos from my childhood. In it was the only picture of me as an infant. Instead of keeping it with the other albums, I had put it by the chair near the fireplace in our room where I could savor each page over and over again.

"Yes," I lied, my heart sinking to an even deeper place within me than it already was.

"Oh good," she exhaled, filled with relief. "I didn't think you'd leave it behind."

But in the flurry of gathering things, believing it was only a drill, I'd forgotten the album was in our room. I knew one day I'd have to tell her the truth, but that day wasn't it.

Heavy with the knowledge of my mother's thoughtful keepsake being rendered to ash, along with the piano she had given me that she took lessons on as a girl, I wandered toward the master closet in the center of the house that was still partially standing. Some of the clothing remained, but nothing that was worth keeping. Then I slowly moved to the kitchen area. The dishwasher was slightly ajar, probably from the roof falling on it, but certain items that hadn't melted inside survived. One was a coffee cup one of the boys had made for me when he was little. I picked it up and carried it with me as I trudged to where my sink used to be. I had kept a specially etched rock on the windowsill above it, and I summoned the boys to lift the heavy sink off the ground so I could rummage through the ashes and see if the rock still remained. Miraculously, I found it, cracked and missing a piece but intact. I wiped the ashes from it with my thumb to reveal that the break in the stone crept right up to the words imprinted on it: *Trust God.* I clutched the rock carefully against my chest as chills and warmth washed over me at the same time, the penetrating combination that fills you when you sense you've witnessed a miracle. Reveling in what I believed was a message from the divine, I suddenly felt an overwhelming sense of lightness in the dark, that somehow, against all logic in the moment, everything was going to be okay.

The boys split up again and I roamed toward the back where the pool was. Our outdoor furniture had tiny burn holes in the cushions but the aluminum frames had survived. One of our large planter pots, though made of fragile pottery, was salvageable too, so we took those items with us, along with the charred gun, the mug, and the stone that reminded me that in spite of the vast nothingness that surrounded us, the material life that had been diminished to dust, nature always had the power, the necessity, to reseed and rebloom, and in that alone there was hope for a new beginning.

DESPITE THE CONSUMING sense of loss we all felt, an air of togetherness bound those of us who had lost our homes, and our world buzzed with donations and the comfort of strangers reaching out to help. Though I'd felt awkward buying new things, I welcomed the numerous bags of used clothing people lovingly packed and brought to us. Lifting each item from its bag, knowing it had once belonged to someone else and that they had willingly given it away in our time of need, gave me an immense sense of comfort and gratitude. Someone understood—even if only on a material level—that we had lost everything, and the generosity of others let us know we weren't merely thought of with sadness and then quickly forgotten. It made my heart swell to connect with something in every bag that seemed to suit me perfectly without the giver knowing it, gifting me with a forever treasure, before I passed the rest on to others.

And the generosity didn't stop there. Maripat threw a party for us and asked every guest to bring a gift card. I think I received $5,000 in various gift cards that day. Businesses made goodwill donations of everything from appliances to furniture to clothes; Macy's and other large stores gave us huge discounts on just about everything. Early on, we didn't have space for anything substantial, but knowing these items were available to us made us feel appreciative and valued. Jeff's wife, Jan, offered us their guest house if we wanted it, with no pressure to accept, promising she wouldn't offer it to anyone else while we took our time deciding. Though we ultimately chose to stay in the hotel—which they generously comped—until we found a temporary home, it took a certain pressure off, knowing we had a place to go if it came down to that.

Our biggest priority became finding a house to rent, but even that didn't last long. Friends of ours, whose house was spared, had a friend who owned a small condo in La Jolla Village. The woman didn't know us, but she offered us her place for a week for free while we pondered our options. We ended up renting it from her for four months.

As we strove to put our lives back together in small pieces, Maripat encouraged me to shop for new things. But somehow, with our lives feeling so temporary in the condo, I couldn't bring myself to think about decor for our future home—or even accumulating things we needed. It's difficult to describe how I was feeling, but I believe that subconsciously, I knew that one day we'd be settled again, and that was the time I'd feel right about rebuilding our lives in a material way. Until then, I simply didn't want to amass more stuff chosen from a place that was traumatized and broken; I wanted to wait until that part of my life—our home—could be re-created with meaning from my heart.

I also had to be gentle with myself: I quickly realized that for every item that could be easily repurchased, there seemed to be one that could never be replaced, something precious from the boys' childhoods, gifts from cherished people, photos and art and books that were unique or unrepeatable . . . items that would pop into my mind one at a time, like individual time-released blows meted out by a tormenting force, some bringing me to my knees with sadness. It's mind-boggling to think of the thousands of objects you own that you can't possibly recall until something triggers them. Yes, insurance would pay for new appliances and furniture and technology and decor, possibly giving me the chance to finally create a home from scratch that truly suited me when the time was right. But it could never bring back the items that were consumed by the dragon that tore through our neighborhood on that October night, and that was what haunted me beyond anything else.

In an attempt to anchor me in a happy past, my sister Patti gave me a bag of things reminiscent of our growing up, which included an unexpected treasure: a cross of tiny mosaics from a trip to Italy our grandmother had made in the 1960s. It had hung on the wall everywhere we lived growing up and I had always found it comforting. Shortly after, my parents sent me the family nativity scene in time for Christmas, the one we carefully set up every year in our living room as kids. Our grandmother had taken another trip abroad in 1961, to Oberamergau, Germany, and had brought the crèche back for us as an heirloom she hoped we would pass down. That mosaic cross and nativity scene, with their sweet origins and warm memories, did more to heal my heart than anything I could have bought in a store. Looking at those items—at their tiny details that held so many recollections of people and places and events that shaped me—I began to realize that who I was materially hadn't completely blown away with the ashes in the wind. To see my history and loved ones manifest in my possessions, however big or small, did my sense of self and my family more good than I ever could have imagined. In a blessed and unanticipated way, those two items were the first blocks of a new foundation of sorts—along with the few albums and keepsakes I had brought with me that fateful night—steadying me during what was inarguably the most unhinged time of my life.

IN THOSE EARLY months, though I was traumatized on multiple levels, most of my discomfort came from having so little around me that was familiar: I wore other people's clothes, sat on other people's couches, cooked with utensils and pots and pans that weren't mine, fumbled around kitchens I didn't know. I felt lucky to have the safety net of insurance, but knowing not everyone who lost their homes had the security we did, I also felt guilty for the time I spent wishing for the comfort of what was. That internal tug-of-war of emotions wore on me, but it also gave me a new and indescribable brand of strength to say no.

My sister Joyce was thoughtful by nature, and with her

heart in the right place, she regularly bought me beautiful things she believed would bring me some measure of joy. But not knowing where I was going and with no solid plan to re-create my life, I simply didn't want the responsibility of random objects I felt no connection to. Normally, it would've been hard for me to turn down these thoughtful gifts, but something in the aftermath of the fire had woven a ribbon of bravery through me. "Thank you," I would frequently say, "but, no." I understood her instinct was to fill me up where she believed I needed filling, and I knew it was difficult for other people to comprehend why a person who had lost everything would reject anything offered to them, but there is a hole too deep to fathom when one's life is reduced to ashes, too complicated to string together into intelligible sentences. Something new can feel like a treat one day and an offense the next. One day, however, Joyce caught me just right and I accepted a beautiful pitcher she had picked out for me. When I used it for the first time, I was glad I was discriminating about saying yes to very few items: the sisterly love that pitcher carried for me was poured into everything I used it for, and I sensed I would feel that way for decades to come.

NOT LONG AFTER we settled into the condo, I received a package. Inside was the blanket made from the boys' tees I had been so adamant about getting to the seamstress on the day of the fire. It hit me then that those plastic tubs I'd pulled down from the closet that evening, the ones filled with the boys' tiny clothes and shoes, had been victims of the blaze. An intense melancholy swept through me, followed by gratitude that I'd had the chance to see and touch those items one last time. I pulled the blanket from the box and immediately put my face up to it, wondering if the scents of my babies would be there somehow, overwhelmed with gratitude to have this tangible object of "us," especially after all we'd been through. I wanted to wrap myself in it and just let the tears flow. But despite being beautifully done, it was unexpectedly stiff, not soft and cozy like I expected—as if the rigidity of the fabrics reflected the strength I needed now, and the coziness I desired would come later. I realized then I could bemoan that it wasn't exactly what I expected, that I couldn't physically envelop myself in the mementos of my children who were now grown men, but what good would that do? One day I could have it rebacked with a soft, snuggly fabric. Until then, I would focus on the fact that there easily could have been no keepsake blanket of those tender days at all—and on my gratitude that all of the men in my life were present with me, alive and well.

DURING THOSE FIRST few months, the five of us clung to each other; the boys looked to us for reassurance that we would rebuild our lives, and I sought a rhythm that Bruce and I could share. He was preoccupied with the insurance claim, so I strove to counter that with optimism about having a fresh start. People asked if we planned to rebuild in Ramona, but I couldn't imagine being fraught with worry every time the dry winds blew in from the east. Reinventing our lives there, with so much uncertainty and the now-charred memories, felt ludicrous. Plus, our big house in the country was the home we had built to raise our sons in—and that part of our lives was over. David was living independently in Santa Monica, Matt had just graduated from Purdue and had an exciting future ahead of him, and Patrick was midstream in his undergrad, also at Purdue. We never imagined that home we no longer needed would be taken from us so unrepentantly, but now that it had, the 500-square-foot condo we currently resided in felt like plenty to me. So what that there was barely any standing room at Christmas? We celebrated just like always, and I knew in my heart that that was what mattered.

Perhaps most heartbreaking among so much heartbreak was one day making the admission to my mom that I hadn't saved my beautiful album from her after all.

"Oh," she said, looking away quickly and then back at me with a closed-mouth smile. "Well . . . there are things much more important."

Though her words were her usual positive ones, her eyes and body language failed to hide her disappointment.

It didn't help that everything I had lost kept coming to me slowly, each item fitting into a category of feeling nothing, evoking tears, or somewhere in between. But losing that album from my mom carried its own unique devastation that nothing could soften; my sadness was compounded by seeing the sadness in her. Though she never expressed it in words, during the short pauses in our conversations when she took so much care to comfort me, I could feel that she hurt in her own way. In those moments, I could hear God whisper to me that only time could lessen the pain.

Having grown up steeped in the Catholic Church, I wanted to believe that was true.

But time is not only an abstract concept that has no true container, no prescribed end to a period of suffering when anguish suddenly lifts like evaporated fog. It is also fickle. A smile or spark of laughter may creep in one instant, only to feel completely inappropriate in the next. I've found that to be true for everyone during times of grief.

But for me, there was a caveat.

Just when I was beginning to heal and slowly reconstruct what we had lost, hopeful that Bruce and I would move toward each other after an ebb and flow of connection that had punctuated our lives in the prior years, he—like the blaze that fateful night that zig-zagged into the path of our home—took an unexpected turn I never saw coming.

bruce

*A*RE YOU SURE YOU DON'T WANT ANYTHING TO eat?" asked my workmate Rachel.

"I'm sure," I quickly replied. "I'm not hungry."

She cocked her head and raised an eyebrow. At 5'9" I probably didn't weigh 120 pounds and must have appeared near starvation.

"How about a loan until payday?" she offered.

The San Diego sun warmed my back as I shook my head. "Thank you . . . but, no."

"You sure?" she asked, her warm brown eyes conveying her concern.

Forever optimistic and filled with naiveté, I nodded, knowing that payday would be around the corner and I'd be back in the game again before too long.

"All right," she said, dragging out the words with a shrug. "But if you change your mind . . ."

Eleven years older than me, Rachel had become my first friend upon my return to San Diego in 1977. She was non-judgmental and with the perfect amount of compassion, be-friended me like a sister, mothered me just enough, and often looked the other way when she didn't necessarily approve of choices I made.

Nineteen and suntanned, I had recently come back from

Kaneohe, Hawaii, where I had attended the wedding of my older sister Joyce. I had quit my job before leaving, and my roommates had saved my place on the rental lease. Consequently, waiting for me in San Diego was a place to live, but also bills to pay and no job.

The night before I left Hawaii for the mainland, my dad and I were walking along the beach when I tentatively turned to him. "Dad, may I have $100?"

I saw strain and resistance in his strong, handsome face, so I immediately padded my request. "I have bills waiting for me, and if you could help me this one time, I'd be so grateful."

He glanced at the pained yet hopeful look on my face. I knew he felt the pressure of providing for a family of eight, which was why I had gotten a job at the age of fifteen—I never wanted him to have to worry about me. After making my uncharacteristic request, I saw him weighing his generous nature with his reluctance to dole out money every time one of his kids wanted this or that. Plus, he had just thrown a beautiful wedding for Joyce that I knew made a dent in my parents' savings. He looked away and gave it some thought.

"Okay," he finally said, reluctantly pulling out his wallet and handing me the bills.

I thanked him sincerely, but I knew that $100 wouldn't cover everything, so I decided to approach my sure thing: my grandparents. They were still staying in the guest house of my parents' oceanfront quarters, and they had always been there for me in a most comforting way. When I showed up and asked them for $100 worth of help, they generously offered $200. Hugging them each tightly, I held fast to my innate sense of optimism that it would all work out. I also clung to a thread of childish inexperience that buoyed me with hope and courage.

Truth be told, I'd been baptized into independence at the

age of eighteen with a lot to learn. Six months earlier, after my father had received orders to relocate to Kaneohe Marine Corps Air Station in Hawaii, I overheard a conversation between my parents while I lurked quietly in the hallway, afraid to breathe for fear of being discovered.

"I worry about Mary staying behind alone in San Diego," my dad said, angst lacing his voice. "I'm not sure she's ready."

Always positive, though her answers were not always well thought through, my mom responded with her typical self-assurance. "Mary? Oh, she'll be fine."

Apparently, that was all my dad needed to hear. If he continued to harbor concern, he didn't express it further. In a show of solidarity with my mother, he and I, along with my younger brother David, went out the following weekend and found a studio apartment for me in La Jolla for $125 a month. It may not sound like much in today's market, but at the time, it was a lot for a young girl on her own for the first time.

Eight months later, with this trip to Hawaii under my belt and two donations in my pocket, I had only a little more than the amount due for the bills I had accumulated while at Joyce's wedding. But that didn't matter. As I stepped off the plane that morning and took my first breath of fresh California air, I was ready to take on the world that lay ahead.

Now that Joyce was married—and even though I now lived in a shared apartment—I felt I was on my own. Joyce and I had always been close, but now she had a husband and a whole new set of responsibilities. So although I had no idea where I was going or how I would get there, I did know I needed a job. Looking back, I'm amazed that with so little post–high school education, I was able to land a job at Pacific Bell. Within less than a week of arriving back in San Diego, I was gainfully employed as a district manager's assistant.

In no time, I was again nearly broke, but I had my '66 VW Bug that ran well enough to get me from Pacific Beach to downtown B Street every day. Though I worked in the Union Bank Building, the cheapest parking I could find was blocks away, so I always had to arrive early enough to hoof it the rest of the way to the office. Even then, the one dollar a day parking fee was a struggle; in fact, I have no recollection of how I managed that daily fee on my minimal salary of $550 a month.

But there I was, though scarcely able to afford food, enjoying my lunch hour outside with Rachel. My stomach may have been grumbling, but being with Rachel lifted my spirits. She also represented a constant, sparkling model of the life I desired.

A military wife, Rachel's husband David picked her up in a new beige Volvo every day after work. The first time I saw him jump out of the car, I was struck by how his Navy Commander uniform matched the color of their car exactly. In a flash, I pictured his handsome, patriotic look making the perfect car advertisement. I also intuitively felt a kinship to them both. At those chance sightings after work, I saw the kind of connection between two people that I wanted to have one day.

The following Saturday, I sat on the steps of my apartment, the sun caressing me with its rays, as I awaited a call from a man I'd recently met. When the call never came, I lamented being "stood up," and I still hadn't shaken it by the time Monday morning rolled around. When I sulked into work, Rachel read my crestfallen face and sidled up a little closer to me than normal.

"You don't look so happy today," she said. "How was your weekend?"

"I'm fine," I said with feigned gusto, forcing a smile so my true feelings wouldn't show.

Rachel took a beat to respond. "Okay, Mary. But I'm here in case you want to talk about it."

As she turned to leave, I grabbed her arm. "I got stood up on Saturday."

A sympathetic look crossed her face. "It happens," she said with a friendly shrug. "Maybe he wasn't the right guy for you."

I felt the sting of tears as her caring tone enveloped me. "That's a good way to look at it," I managed from my nineteen-year-old worldview.

Rachel nodded. "I've found it's usually true."

I looked away and took a deep breath, then peered up at Rachel. "I'm just not sure I'll ever find the kind of guy you have in your life."

Rachel tipped her head playfully. "Welllll . . . maybe I can help."

"Really?" I said a bit too eagerly, feeling the pressure in my chest ease up.

"Yeah . . . David works with a Navy pilot who's new in town. He said he'd love to meet someone. Maybe you'd consider going out with us. I know blind dates can be stressful, but best case you'll like him and worst case it'll be a fun night with David and me. What do you think?"

I'd only had one blind date before. I was sixteen and his name was Jim Snow. I'd had a quiet laugh when he showed up dressed in white from head to toe (how apropos for a guy named Snow!), but despite his curious style, I had a fabulous night. We fell into easy conversation for hours, and I imagined how wonderful it would be to spend more time together. As I looked across the table at him, my heart actually ached knowing I'd probably never see him again. My dad had just been assigned a new duty station in Washington, DC, and we were leaving first thing in the morning. As we said our goodbyes, I thanked him for being a great first blind date, then disappeared into the house wondering if I'd ever have that same luck again.

Maybe it was the kick in my ego or Rachel's gentle understanding, or even the memory of that night when I was sixteen giving me hope, but I agreed to the blind date the following Friday night, which just happened to be April Fools' Day.

ON THURSDAY DURING my lunch break, I walked to one of the modest stores nearby and bought a $19 dress—one that was barely cheaper than my $20 per month parking fees. The next evening, I went over to David and Rachel's where I changed from my work clothes into my new dress, gave my eyelashes a few swipes of mascara, ran a brush through my casually styled, sun-bleached hair, and gave myself a squirt of my favorite perfume, Cachet.

When Bruce arrived at their house shortly after, I was wowed by the tall, slim gentleman who flashed a winning smile at me as Rachel introduced him. His tan skin, combined with his light hair, highlighted his stunning crystal blue eyes, which exuded a confidence I couldn't help but admire.

"Everyone have a seat," David offered.

I had figured that even if the date was a dud, I was sure to enjoy the company of David and Rachel and have a nice dinner out. My paychecks had started coming in by then, but I wasn't going to steakhouses on any regular basis. It wasn't long, though, before my expectations about how the night might go went up a notch.

After about half an hour of casual conversation, Rachel

announced that we should head to the restaurant. Throughout the meal, Bruce gave me every indication that he was interested in me, asking me questions about all kinds of things and displaying the same genuine curiosity he had back at the apartment. So, after we finished eating, I was delighted when he suggested we all go to the Officer's Club in Point Loma, which was the only place in town where a not-yet twenty-one-year-old could get in. Being someone who was always looking for that kind of good time—and being the only underage member of our foursome—I thought he was a genius.

We walked into the club and found a table. Then, Bruce led me onto the dance floor. Swaying in his arms, I immediately felt like I was home.

"You enjoying yourself?" he asked.

"Very much," I said, breathing in his cologne and his strong, yet gentle manner.

The ensuing couple of hours melted away as we fast- and slow-danced to every kind of song the band played. Finally, David sauntered up and suggested we go back to their place. As we strolled out of the club, I looked to my left and saw the familiar blue-starred dome of the church across the street: St. Charles Borromeo. I had attended mass there with my family during our duty station in San Diego in 1974, and I felt a bit of nostalgia fill my heart. I also allowed myself a brief but vivid young girl's fantasy of walking down the aisle of that church with the handsome man on my arm that night.

THE FOLLOWING TUESDAY found me with waning hope that I would hear from Bruce, wondering if perhaps I'd read our connection wrong. *Oh, well,* I thought, trying to skirt my disappointment. *Maybe I was an April Fool after all.*

In those days, technology didn't offer much in the way of instant contact with someone. Because potential relationships were nurtured by phones that connected to a wall, it was more like "the waiting game" instead of "the dating game." Knowing someone's work schedule, and timing a call to their estimated arrival home, was part of the unwritten but predictable set of social rules people went by. Because an entire weekend had passed with me waiting at home for Bruce's call, and then a full two workdays on top of that, I was becoming inclined to think that I hadn't been as captivating as I imagined.

But on Wednesday night, not long after arriving home, my phone rang. It could have been anyone, I knew, but I coated my hello with a little more pizzazz than usual.

"Hello, Mary? It's Bruce."

"Oh, hi," I said, trying to cloak my animation with a nonchalant air.

"How was your day?" he asked, his voice brimming with warmth, confidence, and apparent interest.

"Good. It was good. How was yours?"

"Fine."

We both paused.

"I was wondering," he said, "what are you doing this Saturday?"

"Nothing. Why?"

"I thought you might like to join me on my friend's sailboat. We're meeting at the dock at 10:00."

Right away I panicked. "Oh," I muttered, "actually . . . I forgot. I have to get my car fixed at 10:00."

"Okay," he said.

"Thanks, anyway," I mustered.

"Well, I guess I'll just talk to you later."

With barely a chance to respond to his swift reply, he hung up. No sense of rejection. No apparent concern. I wasn't sure what to make of it. Perhaps worse, I did like the idea of another date with Bruce, and my shy demeanor felt out of character to me. I stared at the phone and wondered why I had made up a lie.

When the phone rang not ten minutes later, it startled me to hear Bruce's voice on the other end.

"Hi, it's Bruce again. My buddy said the afternoon works just as well for him and the others. Can I pick you up at 3:00?"

There was something about his willingness to overlook the brush-off I'd given him that appealed to me. It was then that I realized his abrupt departure from our prior call hadn't been because he was put off, but rather from a desire to alter the plan to a viable one—and fast. Even better, it seemed that my awkwardness wasn't an issue for him. I warmed up to the connection we both seemed to feel and was thrilled that he wanted more of it. We were going on a real date!

The rest of the week flew by and I leapt out of bed early on Saturday morning, eager to get ready for our afternoon together. A stunning blue cloudless sky complemented the soft sway of the palm trees as I busied myself around my apartment. I kept glancing at the clock, then at myself in the mirror, wanting to be sure I looked nice for him.

Right on time, Bruce rapped on the door. I opened it to find him looking handsome as ever. I liked the casual way he was dressed compared to our blind date—though I was quickly learning that nothing about Bruce was particularly casual. I had noticed when we met how thoughtful and deliberate he was about everything he said. At first I wondered if it was because he was trying hard to impress me, but it didn't take long to discover that that was simply Bruce's personality.

"Hi, Mary," he said. "Are you ready to go?"

"I am," I said, grabbing my new blue-tinted aviator sunglasses, which was all that my low-maintenance style at nineteen required.

Bruce escorted me out to his new brown Corvette, then we made our way down to Harbor Island. At one of the stoplights, I looked over at his face and a warm feeling about him washed over me. The memory is as clear today as it was on that April day over forty years ago. I particularly remember the way the sun reflected a ray that lit up his smile, betraying that his teeth were slightly imperfect—yet somehow perfect to me.

WE MET THE group in the crowded Harbor Island rental slip, and after a brief round of introductions, someone pointed. "There she is."

The white sailboat with accents of blue that matched the springtime sky was bobbing up and down on the sun-glistened water, and I felt excitement well up in me. I so enjoyed the fresh air and sunshine, and I felt certain it was going to be a fun afternoon.

After sailing around the bay for an hour, drinking beer, and listening to stories of aviation and military dreams, we pulled up to the pier outside Anthony's Restaurant on the Embarcadero. One of the couples included another nineteen-year-old girl named Amy. When the waitress came to the table, both Amy and I ordered a drink as the others had.

"ID, please?" the waitress stated in the perfunctory manner I had come to learn meant "no drink for this minor."

"Oh, sure," I said, fumbling over my words as I reached into the pocket of my jeans to pull out an ID I knew wasn't there. My breaths were quick and shallow as I felt the blush on my cheeks burn.

"I must have left my ID in the car," I remarked with feigned innocence. "I'll just have a Diet Coke."

Amy, my new equally illegal friend, followed my lead. "I'll have a Diet Coke too."

Laughter circled the table, then the awkward moment passed as abruptly as it began.

After dinner, we resumed our slow, breezy route along the San Diego Bay back to our cars, which included an easy trek past the Coronado Air Station. Parked along the water's edge, in all her grandeur, was an aircraft carrier. I don't remember which one it was specifically, but what I do remember is that it was monstrous and captured everyone's attention. At the time, I didn't realize that a ship exactly like that—only nuclear powered—would be LTJG Bruce Odgers's home in not more than a year.

I also had no idea what that assignment would mean.

WE SETTLED AS a group to admire the scenery. Bruce sat next to me in a sideways sitting position with one leg stretched out straight, the other bent underneath him, as the twinkling lights off the long arch of the Coronado Bridge in the distance framed our perspective. I relaxed into his semi-embrace, not minding the closeness of his arm around my shoulder as we listened to flight stories that he and the other pilots told. He occasionally left my side to get another drink, and I could see that the alcohol gradually relaxed him more. Although I noticed the effects on him, I wasn't troubled by it at the time; if red flags were waving, I completely missed them. Growing up in a military family, regular drinking was part of our culture, so Bruce's behavior while slightly intoxicated was normal to me. What's more, alcohol tended to unlock the door to relaxation and fun for the stressful, highly focused life of a military aviator, so social drinking was both expected and accepted.

What was odd, however, was that each time Bruce's increasingly wobbly legs took him to get another drink, he never offered one to me. In every other way, Bruce was packaged in manners and understated refinement—opening my car door, including me in conversations, giving me his undivided attention. I thought it should naturally follow that he would make sure I, too, had something to drink. Even though I'd possibly embarrassed him at the restaurant and couldn't order something alcoholic, offering me at least some type of beverage would have been nice. Instead, he was focused solely on himself and on his own enjoyment. At the time, however, I was too young and naive to fully recognize that I was negligibly missing from his radar.

BY THE TIME we disbanded, Bruce was obviously in no shape to drive. To my relief, he willingly handed me the keys to his Corvette. Feeling like a true grown-up with a stylish sports car, I slid behind the wheel and drove us to his apartment.

Even at the young age of nineteen, I marveled when I observed things that looked like coincidences. I had come to believe that they only occurred when it mattered and when a particular moment welcomed them. Such was the case when Bruce opened the door to his apartment.

After he flipped on the lights, I stood there stunned.

In the small room were beautiful couches. *My* couches.

Well, not exactly *mine*, but the identical beige and white diagonal-patterned pieces I had picked out but not yet purchased.

"These are the same couches I chose," I exclaimed.

"What do you mean, you chose?" he asked, clearly delighted by my approval.

Believing I was witnessing God's hand in our connection, I felt my heart swell.

"We like the same things," was all I could manage.

Most girls revel in the idea of meeting her Prince Charming, and in that moment, it truly felt like I had. Not only was I filled with unprecedented butterflies, but I wanted to dance, sing, even shout: "It's happening!" I wanted to declare to Bruce that we were connecting in that special way that speaks of tomorrow and the next day and the next, but instead, I played it as cool as a nineteen-year-old girl can.

"Want to see some old photos?" he asked.

"Sure," I said as he led me to one of the magical couches.

He slid an album out from the shelf under the coffee table and cracked it open. Photos of his growing-up years in Edmond, Oklahoma, greeted me, painting the picture of a happy childhood with slightly older, conservative parents, a home on acreage, and a solid, midwestern upbringing with three brothers: Alan, Rob, and John.

At the beginning of the album, they were little boys playing with neighborhood friends, often on horseback. They projected camaraderie with just enough mischief thrown in to capture my interest. As only a photograph can convey, the foursome struck me with their "we can take on the world" look.

"With four sons, you'd think there would've been the occasional trouble," Bruce said, "but there really never was." He continued to describe his family with pride as he turned the pages.

"My parents love music and the theater. We also went to

church every Sunday and were pretty involved in it. They've always had a very strong faith."

I nodded and smiled, in awe at what seemed to be an idyllic upbringing. While I didn't see peaks of excitement in the photographs, I didn't see signs of dramatic dips either. It was simply an old-fashioned kind of happy presented within the atmosphere of a devoted couple's plan to raise four respectful, ethical, well-reared children.

In contrast to the tumultuous, often emotional home I grew up in, I took notice of the type of stability Bruce had come from. It was nothing like the life I'd had that was spiked with giant highs and plunges into constricting lows. The straight line he seemed to be raised on resonated with me, and I was drawn to what that life could look like if I were living it too.

Bruce interrupted my thoughts, pointing to a particular picture of his father. "My dad retired after twenty-five years of service with Western Electric. He was sixty-one."

Still caught up in the striking differences in our childhoods, I offered a perfunctory response to keep the conversation going. "Oh, really? What did he do with his time?"

"All us kids had moved out by then. But they had a big garden Dad loved to work in, and like I said, he and Mom were a big part of the church community."

It wasn't odd back then for someone to retire at sixty-one, and Bruce didn't offer any concerning reasons why he had. So I merely continued to smile as Bruce flipped the pages to reveal himself and his brothers becoming college kids, standing around airplanes and fast cars, taking on the world.

By eleven o'clock or so, Bruce's alcohol buzz wore off enough to drive me back to Pacific Beach. Alone in my apartment, I basked in the happy feeling of the day; my sun-kissed cheeks from the hour on the boat had left me with a warm glow—and though I wasn't thinking too far ahead, I did hope for more time with Bruce. I had no idea that on that night, he had indeed introduced me to my future.

AS THE WEEKS of our relationship turned into months, I was thrown into a different world, one where I began to experience the ebbs and flows of Bruce's personality. The easygoing line that had spelled safety and security to me in his photo album shifted to a zigzag that I found hard to anticipate. It was nothing urgent; just a definite change in his moods in reaction to different events in his life I had yet to experience with him.

Bruce's time at North Island Navy base was filled with intense responsibility. As the pilot of the newly commissioned S-3A—a jet version of the former S-2—Bruce and his crew were tasked with tracking the Russian submarines that lingered off the western coast of the US. As a result of this highly confidential and stress-laden task, Bruce would often be quiet, preoccupied, and disconnected from me, leaving me feeling as if I was on the outside of his private world. While I understood his concerns about landing on a postage stamp in the ocean with only the moon and stars to light his path, he kept his strain bottled up instead of sharing it with me. Feeling alienated while also being immensely drawn to him wasn't the most favorable combination, but being a military kid, I knew the territory came with its ups and downs, so I tried to understand.

During this time, my dad—who was commanding general of the Kaneohe Marine Corps Air Station—would hop a flight across the Pacific in an F-14 to visit his three California daughters. He'd joke about me dating a "sailor," but I knew that as a career infantry officer, he was intrigued to have a naval aviator in the family.

When Dad finally met Bruce, I could tell that he had expected someone a little more cavalier than the highly focused, deliberate person he met. Bruce favoring the maverick type, they took to each other immediately. I saw this as my open door to confide in my dad about Bruce's behavior and perhaps get some advice.

"Do you have any idea what this man is carrying on his shoulders?" my dad barked as only a Marine general could. "Not just anyone can develop the skill and precision needed to accomplish a feat like that."

Used to his directness, I merely said, "Hmmm, you're right. I get it."

Choosing a partner who was an officer in the military had its responsibilities and perks, its drawbacks and burdens. I had momentarily forgotten the undying support I had witnessed my mother provide as a military wife. Married to a Marine officer for nearly twenty-five years, she not only mastered but truly loved the empathetic, accepting life of the military spouse. The question was: could I provide the same?

Without a pause, I knew I could.

I had enormous admiration for Bruce. I saw him as the best of the best in his S-3 Red Griffin squadron, where he was known by his call name, BK—his first two initials. His conscientiousness ruled everything he did both professionally and personally. With a certain grace, he carried the risks of a demanding profession—and I unwittingly took on that tension in our life together. The lighthearted ways of a woman seven years his junior only served to magnify that tension. The truth was, I felt like, and was viewed by others, as an old soul in a young girl's body, and consciously or not, I observed in Bruce a quiet, controlled demeanor that seemed to crave my unbridled spirit. He loved being with my family and their endless antics, and he always excelled at calming the emotional upheavals that interacting with them often had on me. Sometimes, compared to his closely managed self-control, I looked like a psychological project! But the differences in us seemed to create a balance that formed a desire for each other that turned into love.

When Bruce was assigned to be a jet pilot in the Indian Ocean, landing regularly on an aircraft carrier, I was thrilled he was able to make time to write me daily letters. It didn't take long before he became my world, and when I got word from a military friend that he was shopping for a diamond in Hong Kong, I was elated.

Weeks later, I drove up to meet the ship as it glided into the Alameda harbor on its return to American waters, brimming with anticipation. After seven months of writing letters and an occasional phone call, Bruce had become a part of me, and I realized I truly loved him. So when he asked me to marry him that evening and presented me with a sparkling solitaire, I threw my arms around him with an enthusiastic yes.

That night, lying in bed with the ring on my finger and a million thoughts swirling in my head, I couldn't fall asleep. I was grateful my future with Bruce was certain and I would be accompanying him to his next duty station. In more ways than not, he was the man of my dreams and I was eager for this new chapter. I couldn't imagine meeting anyone I loved more, so I ignored the words of my parents echoing in my mind—that there was no reason to get married so young—and began making plans for our wedding.

❧

BRUCE AND I began our life together as newlyweds with an unexpected but welcome assignment: orders to the Training Command in Pensacola, Florida, where Bruce would fly a jet called a T-2 as an instructor.

Not only would we be living in a beautiful city, but a lovely home with a big yard was waiting for us when we arrived. We adopted a dog. I got a job. Months later, we celebrated our first anniversary on the white sands of Pensacola Beach.

A year and a half into our tour, Bruce had earned enough flight hours to be competitive, so he applied for a job with Delta Airlines. Soon after, I stood on the tarmac, adjacent to the hangar that housed the training jets at Pensacola Air Station, waving a white envelope above my head. "It's a letter from Delta," I yelled through the hot and muggy late summer day.

I could see Bruce in the distance, tall and lean in his military green flight suit and black boots. He broke into a run and we embraced in the sheer exhilaration of the moment, as his lofty goal of being a Delta pilot morphed further toward reality.

He carefully opened the envelope with the red-and-blue symbol engraved on the return address to find notice of the psychological evaluation, the highly anticipated second step in the interview process. It was almost viewed as a formality— once you got that far you were all but in—but outside the final physical examination, it was a necessary link in the process of being hired by Delta.

Not long after, in early fall of 1981, Bruce passed both exams and bid goodbye to six years of Naval service. He had served them with pride, and the Navy had served him with the excellence required to now join a commercial airline and the prestigious Delta family.

After completing training at Hartsfield International Airport in Atlanta, Georgia, we chose the Delta base that was closest to California—the one in Plano, Texas, a suburb of Dallas/Fort Worth International Airport. Bruce started as a flight engineer, third man in the cockpit, of a Boeing 727. And within a year, we started the family we both desperately wanted.

꒰ঌ

AFTER EIGHT AND a half years of Bruce being a pilot for Delta, and being blessed with our boys, at times it was like being a single mother with Bruce gone so much. Raising three children for chunks of time on my own was admittedly difficult, but at the same time, the boys and I developed a special bond—a certain subculture that buzzed with our own dynamic. While the boys loved their father and Bruce certainly adored his children, when Bruce was home, that dynamic in our home shifted. It's not that it was bad or good, just different. My energy was quite different from Bruce's, and the boys and I had a particular routine. So as a natural consequence, we developed two distinct family vibrations: one with the rhythm of the four of us, and another that hummed among all five. It took a silent adjustment on my part each time Bruce returned from a stint away, but the one thing that never wavered was my devotion to my sons' receiving the best of both of us.

Growing up, my parents were completely focused on my father's military career. As a result, we felt loved but sometimes not like a priority; my dad was most often the one in the spotlight, thriving on building a successful career. I didn't want any of my children to feel that sense of living under a shadow, so I threw myself into hands-on, love-centered motherhood, and I loved every minute of it.

The problem was, I no longer wanted to live in Texas. I had made the best of it for nearly a decade, and although Bruce and I both agreed that we wanted to return to San Diego to raise our sons, Bruce felt it was simply too expensive. He had always been cost conscious, but it had escalated over the years to downright frugality.

"How about we make a list of why we should go and why we should stay here in Texas," I persisted.

Bruce let out a frustrated sigh, but I made the list anyway.

Pros	*Cons*
fresh air	*cost of moving*
access to nature	*real estate too expensive*
proximity to the ocean	*long commute to LAX*
being near the mountains	
ability to transfer to LAX	

The "want to" won over the "should" list, and it wasn't long before we were on our way west. Little did I know, the unheard, yet-to-be identified part of Bruce's reluctance to move was the beginnings of the pressure he carried—a pressure that our new home, increased expenses, and maturing family would, in time, exceed my husband's ability to carry.

SHORTLY BEFORE OUR tenth wedding anniversary in February of 1989, we found the 9.3 acres in Ramona, California, that impelled us to further ignore our pro and con list.

I had no idea that the home we would build and expect to live in forever would last only fifteen years—and that almost every material thing I treasured would be reduced, along with Bruce's state of mind, to nothing but a pile of ashes.

❧

AFTER THE FIRE, in 2007, when the five of us moved into the 500-square-foot condo in La Jolla Village, the cramped living conditions compared to those of our big house actually afforded a certain coziness to me. But as the weeks passed, instead of sharing my love for our space, Bruce felt more and more hemmed in.

Not long before we lost our house, Delta filed bankruptcy, and Bruce had agonized for weeks over whether to leave. Once he made the decision—perhaps the toughest he'd ever made— he was hired by a millionaire to be his private pilot. At first, Bruce enjoyed the jaunts to various places, but before long, the man called on Bruce less and less, which meant Bruce was relegated to our dimly lit condo more and more. Though the man still paid him, Bruce liked order and a timetable he could count on; he also thrived within a demanding schedule. So the long periods of not being needed as a pilot inflicted an intense unrest in him. In an attempt to counter it, he determined that our insurance adjustor wasn't doing what he was hired to do— though with polite humor, the adjustor made it clear that Bruce didn't need to be spending time and energy doing his job —and threw himself into documenting our life nail by nail for hours on end for the insurance company. His need to be in control of a largely out-of-control life at that time completely consumed him, until I finally realized he couldn't go on in that little condo any longer.

I didn't want to move; I'd been uprooted too many times and found it difficult to keep up with my fluctuating emotions. But once I saw the place Bruce found—and knowing we had an allotment for higher rent from the insurance company—I softened. Though the view of the ocean was partially blocked, the home was right on the bluff, and the road that led to it was breathtaking. So we packed our meager belongings and moved up the coast to Del Mar into a 3,000-square-foot townhouse where we all, Bruce especially, could breathe.

Having been through such a whirlwind of devastation and loss, I chose to see our new surroundings as a literal breath of fresh air, filled with promise for our new start. But once again, instead of embracing it the way I did, Bruce merely continued on his trajectory of getting our life back in order through hours of calculating and documenting and calculating again. It didn't help that in 2008, the stock market took a terrible downturn, and Bruce added perseverating over the daily results of the S&P to his list of compulsions. I got to the point where I'd ask him to promise not to check our plummeting retirement accounts while I was at work. All of it affected his mood negatively, which of course affected mine.

But then, what he believed was an excellent investment opportunity came our way. Though he'd never asked me to be involved in the financial side of our affairs, he presented the details to me and asked what I thought. Thrilled that Bruce had actually asked for my advice, I sat down with him and looked carefully at the possibility we'd been presented with. We agreed it was a risk, but the man was a friend, and we had every hope that we could recover a nice chunk of money by investing in him.

Only the "friend" turned out to be a sociopath, and the deal a complete lie.

Soon after we made the investment, I walked into the

kitchen to find Bruce standing stock still. This man who had always been on top of his game in his profession, who had thrived under the expectation of never making a mistake, looked completely empty with defeat.

"He stole the money from me," he said.

"What?" was all I could manage.

I wanted to ask a dozen questions, but I saw my husband unraveling in front of my eyes and instead walked over to comfort him. It had been awhile since we'd embraced, and I was startled to feel the skin and bones that comprised the shell of the man he'd become. For one of the first times in our marriage, I knew Bruce was swimming in a pool of vulnerability when his sad voice uttered, "That feels so good."

I didn't know it in the moment, but I believe it was my first glimpse of what was for Bruce the last and final straw.

ON OCTOBER 13, 2008, Bruce dropped David off at the movies, then went to run some errands. By the time I came home from work around 5:00, David was there and told me he'd gotten lost on his way back to the condo, that he'd called his dad for help, but that Bruce hadn't offered to pick him up, only gave him further verbal directions.

Bruce had always been a nurturing father and never missed an opportunity to meet David's sometimes special needs—which included his inability to drive due to visual limitations—so I found it perplexing that he'd left our son in the lurch and was staying out late for no apparent reason.

When Bruce didn't return by 7:00, I texted. *No response.* I called his cell phone. *No answer.* I left a message asking where he was and telling him we'd wait to have dinner with him.

But hours passed and he still didn't show up, nor did he call. By that time I was consumed with worry and left yet another message. Finally, I received a text that simply said, "I just need some space."

For a full hour after that, we texted back and forth, with me cajoling and begging him to call me. When my phone finally rang and Bruce's voice met mine, I could hear my heart pounding in my ears as I felt my mouth go dry.

"Where are you?" I wanted to know, my hands trembling as the words tumbled out in a voice I hardly recognized as my own.

He was in a hotel room, he said, but he refused to tell me where. "It's not far from home," he assured me.

From the few words he spoke, I could immediately read that he was having a major breakdown. All the emotions of fight or flight vibrated through the line as he told me he had taken off the wrong way from the runway of his last trip.

"What do you mean, the 'wrong' way?" I asked, confused.

The man for whom he flew the private plane parked his jet in a small airfield that didn't always have an air-traffic controller, so if something wasn't executed perfectly, or something actually went wrong, no one would have known during an unsupervised takeoff or landing.

"I didn't take off into the wind," Bruce said, his words heavy with torment.

"But if there wasn't an air-traffic controller on duty, what's the big deal? If you were in any trouble, I'm sure you would have heard from the FAA by now."

But Bruce was the epitome of precision and of performing every detail of his job with no margin for error. I felt certain it was why he had been selected as the only pilot from his Navy squadron who was hired by Delta. Other pilots were excellent too, but Bruce was exemplary in his work in every sense of the word. He reserved no place within himself to make a mistake, which was why he was a top-tier pilot—and why not feeling in complete control knocked him off his foundation. He simply couldn't bear the notion of having done something wrong, even if he was the only one who knew about it.

"This is awful, how you're feeling right now," I said, knowing Bruce's inability to cope with a mistake. "But I'm sure if there was an infraction committed, not only would your stellar record stand for you, but they would have contacted you by now."

I could almost hear him shaking his head.

For thirty-eight minutes, he belabored the state of his despair using the takeoff incident as evidence. And I, with my signature optimism beginning to fade, did everything I could to convince him that everything would work out, to just come home, that there was nothing that couldn't be solved.

But somewhere in the conversation, I knew I'd lost him.

In hindsight, I shouldn't have been surprised; I'd rarely had success in talking Bruce into anything he was certain of. And that night was no different. When we hung up, I had no idea what might come of his odd behavior, but my gut told me that things were beyond a supposed "wrong takeoff," which was something Bruce simply wouldn't do in his world of unfailingly high standards.

"Okay," I finally said. "I get that you want some time. But if you're not home in thirty minutes, I'm going to call our parents. I'm also going to call the police to come find you."

He agreed, we hung up, and I somehow drifted off to sleep.

Thirty minutes later he called and told me that he couldn't get home within the time frame we agreed on. "Don't call the police," he said. "I'll just be a few minutes longer."

I let out an exhausted sigh that carried a mixture of worry, frustration, and fear. "Okay, then," I told him. "Just be careful and take the time you need. I'll see you soon."

As I collapsed once again into a bone-tired sleep, it dawned on me that it didn't seem like the call came from a car. I immediately sat up and called him back, but the call went straight to voicemail.

WHEN I WOKE up again, a dull light cast an eerie glow into our room. I leapt out of bed and blinked hard as I looked out the window to see the moonset, something I'd never seen before. It struck me as eerie that the blue sky of daytime was juxtaposed against the pink tinge of sunrise. In my half-asleep state, I turned around abruptly to confirm that Bruce wasn't there. Scared to death by the uncharacteristic behavior of my husband, I called the police to file a missing persons report.

When the officer arrived, I was still in my robe. He looked me up and down with a sigh. "So your husband didn't come home last night?" he remarked in a tone that said I was wasting his time, as if he saw me as one of *those* wives. "We don't normally file a report unless it's been twenty-four hours."

"I know," I said, trying to steady my voice and trembling legs. I didn't want to give the cop any more ammunition to peg me as an overdramatic spouse than he already assumed I was.

I ushered him into the kitchen and sat at the table, a numbness burrowing through me as I explained the situation.

"All right," the officer said with another sigh. "I'll make an exception."

After he wrote up the report with a glaring lack of compassion for me, he saw himself out. I called my brother, Michael, and canceled my afternoon with him. The timing was terrible. He had just moved to California that month from North Carolina, where he had caused a devastating car accident that shook our family to the core. I had been one of the few family members to stand by him, and he naturally leaned on me for support. But I couldn't focus on Michael just then. Only I didn't realize that when I didn't give him a reason for my abrupt cancellation, it aroused his suspicion. As he was making calls to alert the family that something was wrong, I was taking my worry out onto the beach, inhaling the salty air as I walked and walked along the shore, wondering where Bruce could possibly be, what was going through his head to make him scare me like this.

I had witnessed his erratic depression intensify over the years, but I had never been able to make it better. His glass was too often half empty, and he missed so incredibly much because of it. He missed the adventures, the spurs of the moment, the impulsiveness of childishness when it was just the two of us. The mysteries of not knowing all the little details, the joy from our various events. He killed the laughter with his worries and overthinking while I took to reading self-help books, offering all kinds of new ideas to bolster and convince him there was pure joy in them—all to no avail.

It was true that my immaturity and occasional temperamental outbursts in our early years pushed him away, but I'd worked hard on myself and felt I'd long ago succeeded in growing up. I believed my desire for closeness with my husband and partnering on life's issues was a reasonable request, yet I was constantly left thinking, *Why don't you just reach out, take my hand, and walk with me? What do you have to lose?* I hated myself for not being successful in reaching him, while at the same time wondered if I was being too hard on myself. He gave me the space I needed to be with friends and do my own thing, which I was glad for; I admit I was happy at times to be away from him and how stuck he was. But the happiness I shared with my friends was a happiness I also wanted to share with my husband. Unfortunately, something held him back, held him closed.

That evening, with still no word from Bruce and with Matt now home keeping vigil with me as David slept upstairs, I headed off to bed around 9:30. As I started up the staircase, a police car pulled up. I turned slowly. Then, like a robot propelled by sheer terror, I walked quickly out the front door and met the officer, a female, on the lawn.

"Please don't tell me my husband . . ." I said as I reached out to her.

With pain in her eyes, she held me up and gently told me the news.

I felt myself separate from my body. Over my shoulder I saw Matthew on the porch steps with a look of horror on his face. His voice seemed to come out in slow motion as his mouth formed the words, "It's okay, Mom, I'll take care of it. I'll take care of it."

But there was nothing to take care of.

Bruce hadn't been in an accident.

He had been found in a hotel room in Hemet, seventy miles from home.

He had taken his own life.

IN THE ENSUING hour, the three of us clung to each other, numb and in disbelief, while the officer sat with us and offered her help. We all felt it was imperative that Patrick find out in person, not through someone else or through social media, so I called Maripat with the horrible news. As if on the wings of angels, she arrived in no time at all. While she made reservations for us to fly to Indiana, David and I numbly sat at the dining room table, listening to the muffled sound of Matt vomiting behind the closed bathroom door.

By 5:00 a.m. we were on our way to the airport to deliver the sickening news to Patrick. The following day, we all returned together to San Diego.

Suddenly, it was the four of us again, as it had once been in the days when Bruce was flying for days or weeks at a time, when that particular dynamic that belonged to only my sons and me wrapped itself around us and buoyed us with its specialness.

But those days were over.

And, unthinkably, Bruce's were as well.

In an attempt to comfort our broken hearts, we spent the next days swimming in the ocean bathed by fall's golden sunlight, and the boys lay on the floor of my room until I fell asleep at night. It was unspeakable, what had happened, and none of us knew quite how to articulate what we were feeling. After the realization sank in that Bruce had chosen to take himself from us willingly, we felt everything from confusion to guilt to anger to heartbreak. There was simply no soothing balm to apply, no answers to our questions. We were together in our grief, yet each alone in it too.

We planned Bruce's funeral in a daze, as if checking priorities off a list. Cremation. Urn. Flowers. Music. Photo or no photo? What should the program say?

People drifted in and out. Friends I thought I could count on, including one as dear to me as a sister, soon disappeared, seemingly unable or unwilling to deal with some of the choices I made in my brokenness. One couple, relatives, who had to travel for the funeral arrived with the assumption that staying with us was perfectly acceptable and wouldn't be an imposition. I wanted to say no, but I didn't have the courage. What made it worse was that the wife acted like *she* was the grieving widow at the funeral home, while the husband remained detached, ignoring everyone's emotional state. I was dumbstruck, but what could I say? The only thread of strength I possessed was for holding my family together. And it wasn't their lack of sympathy or social grace that floored me, it was discovering that they weren't actually there to support our family; they were merely interested in carefully collecting evidence on "what really happened."

But they were definitely an exception. Most people stepped in to hold me up in ways I wouldn't have expected. One angel, a neighbor of fifteen years, made it a point of telling me I was amazing for braving this inconceivable storm, empowering me to keep taking steps forward with her specific brand of perpetual kindness. Until she told me that, I had no idea how much I needed to hear it. And more than one person actually gently told me that Bruce had given me the best gift by leaving. They had seen me struggle in his shadow, observing from the outside how Bruce—though he didn't mean to hold me back—hadn't known how to let me shine in my own light.

And the boys, they were no longer children nestled in their childhood rooms awaiting story time or goodnight kisses or anything that resembled life as they knew it. Patrick had to return to school, David and Matthew to their adult lives. Before I knew it, I was on my own again, trying to connect the pieces of how Bruce had come to this final, unimaginable decision.

I'd felt apprehension the night we got engaged. *Why?* Was it youth or did I have concerns about Bruce's dad and his reaction to stress, that though controlled, may have caused him to retire early? Was there more to it than I realized? Had Bruce unwittingly worried about the same type of unrest happening in his career as a pilot? When the crook took us for all that money, Bruce had said, "He stole from me." Not *us. Me.* Had Bruce taken it so personally that he couldn't bear not having seen through a man he thought he could trust?

Bruce definitely had a social relationship with alcohol, one that taunted him like an enemy he sometimes found difficult to refuse—one that he used as a crutch to offset his stress. He was always functional, but in our thirty years together, I saw alcohol distance Bruce from us plenty of times, altering his speech, coordination, and mood, and even adding to his air of depression the day after. So it was no surprise that an empty bottle was found in the hotel room where Bruce took his last breath. How much difference had that alcohol made in his decision to end his life?

Years ago, when Bruce had some abnormal cells come back from a prostate screening, he took it on like a disease that had already settled into his body, one he had to cure, to control. It was typical of him to take certain situations and expand them into something that wasn't real, and that was a perfect example. It didn't matter that the doctor had told him it wasn't unusual for cells to show up that way from a screening, and that prostate cancer was one of the slowest growing, so there was no cause for worry. But Bruce had to attack it head on. I told him that if he truly was sick, I would take care of him. I had enrolled in nursing school the day Patrick started kindergarten and had worked part-time as a nurse since graduating. In addition, I told him I'd be happy to work full-time and provide health coverage for the family if that was necessary. He simply looked at me with no indication that he was comforted. Had I stepped into that role, I realized it would have upended the stellar mantle he had built of the responsible husband and father, the one who could always be counted on to take care of his family. What would people think of him if he let his wife take care of him and his children? No, *he* was expected to be that person, *always*. Nothing, *nothing* would allow him to shirk that responsibility and possibly be seen in a diminished light by others, perceived or imagined.

At the funeral, when I pulled Bruce's copilot aside and asked about that supposed "wrong takeoff," he shook his head, clearly confused. "I was right there," he said. "Nothing went wrong that day. Bruce would never take off with the wind."

As I reflected on all of these events that wove their way through our relationship like constricting branches of a sinister tree, as I pushed through the myriad emotions I felt, all the sadness and disbelief that my husband of thirty years had come to believe that suicide was his only way out, I had one single resentment toward him, only one: that he couldn't be there to comfort the sons he loved with all his heart when they needed him the most.

Journal Entry

November 28, 2008

Bruce left us six weeks ago—October 14. He ended his pain and started ours. Here's a guy who went out of his way to not hurt anyone—never had cross words, never got in a fight. Where did all that energy go? Did it explode on that early morning in some hotel in Hemet, CA? In some nondescript, out of the way, I don't want to be any trouble, cold and impersonal

*and lonely room so far from our home? He who
never took anything from others took everything from
us on his exit. And now it's our challenge to get back
what we can. It's our challenge to preserve the
remnants of what we were—to rebuild a life from the
shards of broken glass, from the ashes that want to
blow away into eternity and leave us with nothing
but the ugliness of it all. And it is so ugly. Like a flu
that wells up inside us. And it's coupled with the fear
that it's terminal, that we'll never get over it and our
lives really are changed forever.*

*I get moments of a reprieve—moments of clarity
where my fight comes back. No, I wasn't the perfect
wife. Far from it at times but so close in others, and
mostly right in matters of intention. How
incomprehensible that this would be Bruce's choice. I
would have done anything. But his refusal to take
that option was always there between us . . . that
inability to "partner up" with me. And in that, my
frustration grew—and with that, his isolation was
reinforced—and with that, our world shattered into a
million trillion microscopic pieces.*

*And now is the time for new choices. Do we give in
to this paralysis of our hideously damaged spirits?
Or do we begin the impossible journey of finding our
way to the light that I'm sure exists at the end of our
tunnel?*

*I have to help the boys along, but the journey is
ultimately theirs. I've become so critical of them—
their manners at the table, their messiness at home—
meaningless things. Is it because I'm trying to control*

what appears to be an out-of-control world I live in? Or is it that I'm in shock at the flaws of their father and what those inconsistencies have done to us all, and I don't want them to be flawed so I pick at every little thing? The foundation they were raised on fostered laughing at yourself and living with, while working on, fallibilities. Oh God, how I pray they find their way through this nightmare to confidence and belief in self and the courage to push through to the beauty that surely exists in this world. If our perception really is our reality, then our goal is to see ourselves as powerful and capable, and as courageous as the bravest. Instead of discouraging the bad, I make the commitment to encourage the good. There is so very much of it. That's my goal for today, for them and for me. Just for today, I'll encourage the good.

"Circumstances do not determine a man; they reveal him."

Later that same day . . .

Joyce from the RB Winery came and decorated our tree. Matt went with me this morning and we got it out of storage . . .

I became angry after being sad when I came across our stockings. I hung four on the back of the couch and left Bruce's in the plastic bin. It felt awful. I walked on the beach. I wished I could die so I could be with him again. I just felt so awful. He could have fixed things—it was all fixable—or was it? He thought not. He was so wrong. He was so stuck. How *could he think it was hopeless? How could he have been so stuck?*

I just have to walk it off when I feel so angry.

The boys are still hurting but I'm really proud of how they're trying.

There's so much sadness here. It's a sick feeling. When will it end? I hate waking up in the morning knowing I have to face it all day . . .

Patrick leaves for school tomorrow. We're discussing plans for his birthday and our Christmas plans too. It all has an atmosphere of emptiness surrounding it because of Bruce. We'll go through the motions anyway. It's like decorating the living room for Christmas. How can I feel joyful when the burden of Bruce's killing himself weighs so heavily on all of us? How could I have lived with someone for nearly thirty years and not known he was so close to doing something so horrible? I'm appalled at his choice. I'm angry at the world. I fill my days with good people and uplifting things and it helps so much, but when it's over I'm alone again in my misery of sadness, anger, and loneliness.

I know life will get better someday. I just can't handle any more bad things.

I couldn't have known just how many devastating blows were waiting for me right around the corner.

d a d

⁓⁂⁓

$\mathcal{I}$ AM FOUR YEARS OLD. THE NEIGHBOR GIRL ON the base at Camp Lejeune has a gleaming bike that I'm too little to ride. She encourages me to get on it, so I climb up onto the seat behind her with my legs dangling and she starts to pedal. It feels like pure freedom until my foot gets caught in the spokes and I fall to the ground howling. Seemingly in a flash, I feel my father's strong arms scoop me up and rush me into our kitchen. My mother immediately starts treating the wound, but it is the overwhelming feeling of safety that emanates from my father that surrounds me most vividly.

Three years later, when I have yet another bike accident—this one requiring fourteen stitches and leaving me shy two molars—it is again my dad who fills me with a sense of comfort and security. By this time, however, the circumstances are different. With an ice pack held to my bleeding chin and my head still whirling, I want him to scoop me up like he had when I was four, but at seven he sees me as too big to carry—and I know instinctively that he doesn't want to chance blood staining his uniform. Despite that, though, he is the one who lovingly tells me over and over again that everything will be all right. Perhaps it is his years of service as a US Marine Corps officer that equips him to leap to the rescue of the injured. Or perhaps it is the sometimes tender place—in contrast to his stern exterior—that he holds inside for his daughters.

BORN THE THIRD of five children—the first boy after two calm, dependable, and studious girls—David Malone Twomey was, in contrast to his sisters, easily distracted, academically uninterested, and a huge tease among his siblings, causing frequent disruptions for his overwhelmed and temperamental mother. With his father a Navy submariner who spent the majority of his career out to sea, his mother had her hands full and enrolled my father in kindergarten as early as she could, when he was only four. But in her haste to get another child out of the house for half a day, she unwittingly threw her first son into an environment he wasn't ready for. As a result, he had to repeat kindergarten the following year. The shame set in when his mother and other relatives had the audacity to tease him about it, branding him with the belief that he was stupid.

While most people might carry that feeling of inferiority around for decades, my dad instead allowed it to motivate his curiosity, making him a natural cultivator and sharer of information. On a subconscious level, I believe he turned being demeaned into being a person who fervently pursued knowledge and became a thoughtful conversationalist with all people, thereby refuting any notion that he was "less than" on an intellectual level. I also believe that satisfying his insatiable curiosity filled a space inside that was fighting ancestral demons.

Within our family, it was common knowledge that my father's parents had "taken the pledge," which meant that they had sworn off any intake of liquor. This was not because they were staunch prohibitionists back in the 1920s, but because they had witnessed the role alcohol had played in unraveling their families, and they feared what it could do to theirs if they fell prey as their parents had. So my father grew up with sober role models who allowed no alcohol in the house, ever. But by the time he went to college, the pull of his genes and the social pressures got the better of him. He didn't just drink; he drank so excessively that he would stumble loudly into the house at night, waking everyone. His family enabled this routine by turning a blind eye, and my father allowed the feeling of abandon to become like a drug for him. Whatever ate at him from his childhood, whatever stress he felt from his studies, was numbed by imbibing, and it continued after he was commissioned as an officer in the military.

In Marine culture, drinking was part of the brotherhood—a sort of badge of honor the men wore for keeping up with the hardiest among them. Their weekly "mess nights" at the Officers Club, where only men were allowed, fostered a warrior mentality; a highly regarded Marine could not only drink with the best of them, but he could retain his rigorous physical fitness, as well as show up "spit and polished" after a night of inebriety.

My dad mastered all of those feats with flying colors.

Once my parents started having children, it didn't help that my mom was the loose, Bohemian-style parent; she didn't care what chaos we created or if our toys were strewn about everywhere. We were all high spirited and she seemed completely unfazed by that. But my dad hated it. A man of structure and boundaries, our messes and unbridled energy would trigger him—and while he was by no means a drunk, if he'd had his usual evening wind-down drink (or two), he could be unpredictable, sometimes lashing out physically.

By 1963, there were five of us kids, three girls and two boys—Joyce, me, Patty, Michael, and David (my youngest sister Carol would arrive three years later). At the time, my father taught ROTC at Duke University and was diligently studying for his PhD; when he was at home, he was typically holed up in his small office, working on his dissertation. He hated being disturbed when he was researching or writing, and with his office right off the living room and a passel of kids under the age of eight, it was nearly impossible to have complete quiet. But every so often, his door would be partially open and he would be in a mood to chat. On those days, my two sisters and I would calmly appear in the doorway. Although we were only allowed to interrupt him for short bursts of time, it was at that tender age of six that I began to notice how nice it was to engage in conversations with my dad. A good listener who showed genuine interest in us, he loved the engagement of getting reacquainted after a long day of work—and we loved the way it made us feel important in the midst of his life filled with obvious responsibilities.

By the time we were teenagers, we had moved yet again, this time to Washington DC. My dad had put his PhD studies on hold to progress in his military career and was close to becoming a general officer. With the stress level in our home heightened by adolescent drama and growing rambunctious boys, my father often found escape in his second-floor office, where he would read diligently to increase his knowledge base. At that time, we lived in a three-story house, and because the girls' bedrooms were on the third floor, my sisters and I had to tiptoe past his office on the way to our rooms after school, hopeful not to awaken the beast. On occasions, he'd say, "Who's out there?" and our cover would be blown. We'd then have to undergo the routine questioning process. As teenagers, it wasn't as fun as when we were little. Asking what we were doing gave him the connection to us he desired—and ours to him—when we were young, but as we got older we became textbook detached teenagers who wanted their privacy. He didn't like it, but he did his best to control his irritation. Lucky for me, I seemed to be the child who triggered him the least. I guess I learned early on how strong his intolerance was to chaos and disorder after a day of stress, maneuvering through the rigid and obedient world of leading Marines. But my other siblings didn't always operate with the same understanding that I did and some of them caught his wrath on a much more regular basis. Add a drink or two to that and it could, and sometimes did, turn brutal. As I consistently witnessed his untethered beating of my siblings—particularly Patti, who was always a bit unhinged and never failed to do maddening, unpredictable things, and Michael, who unsettled my father as being "different"—for even minor transgressions, I would run and hide in my room, cringing and crying, scared to death. With the echoes of abuse swirling around me like a taunting spirit I couldn't silence, I could feel my respect for my father slowly slipping away.

But it wasn't only my father who rattled me.

When Dad's Irish temper would rage, my mother's complaisance was something I could never come to terms with. During his outbursts, I would cover my ears and wonder, *Isn't Mom upset hearing and seeing her children yelling? Isn't she bothered by Dad hitting us so violently? Why doesn't she defend us?* But my mother's primary goal was to "keep the peace." I know, it makes no sense. My father's lashing out could certainly not be considered peaceful. But she knew she would only make things worse if she tried to stand up to her inebriated or otherwise incensed husband.

And so, such was the dynamic in the Twomey house between my near polar opposite—yet devoted and very much in love—parents and their half dozen spirited offspring.

✢

DESPITE HIS MILITARY sternness and rigid rules, my father wasn't always a despotic and preferably avoided presence; in fact, he had a whole other side to him that we all embraced wholeheartedly. (My mother may have been an exception to this with some of the antics he pulled, but we kids were always game.) When he wasn't absorbed in his work or studies, his love of fun and adventure was contagious and even thrilling at times. Truth be told, I think instilling an adventurous side in us made us more interesting in his eyes. "Come on," he'd say, "let's see who can run around the track the fastest!" Or "Come and sit and I'll quiz you on the state capitals or the presidents!" I remember once going with him to buy a block of ice for our cooler, and on the short ride back, he repetitively timed me to see how long I could hold the block of ice on my bare upper thighs. No matter that my legs got bluer and bluer each time I held it longer. He kept cheering me on, and I kept pushing myself to triumph in his bizarre choice of contests, simply to make him proud.

In what I would call his "reckless yet controlled" manner of operating, he was also keen on introducing elements of amusement that often accompanied the risk of something daring—as if he wanted us to face fear and conquer it. For example, when Joyce and I were about seven and six, we would wait a few houses down on a vacant corner lot for him to drive up from his day at Duke in his red Volkswagen Bug. After a momentary stop, we would hop on the running boards and hold on to the sides of the open window, squealing with childish glee as he slowly drove us home. Or he would lie on his back in the living room or the front yard and say, "Okay, now one of you get up on that chair and then step down onto my feet."

He'd hold our hands to steady us, then he'd let go as he pushed his legs up so that we were standing on his feet up in the air, like a balancing act in the circus. I don't know how many tumbles we kids took off his feet doing that, or how many bruises we ended up with, but I do remember my mother saying, "Now, Dave, someone's going to really get hurt doing that."

But he was unstoppable.

"We're just roughhousing," he'd say. And we kids, caught up in the spirit of his enthusiasm, all played along.

It was during these times that it was hard to reconcile my dad's two wildly different sides. We could have a blast with him in the afternoon, then his mood would change and one or more of us would catch hell in the evening. He especially hated shows of emotion that involved tears—if the waterworks started, you knew the tolerance level on his end would be zero.

Over time, I grew leery of his unpredictable side. If he was up, that energy permeated everyone he came into contact with; if he was in a dark place, he could quickly suck the life from every person in the room. My mother often took the brunt of his harsh words and oscillating disposition, even though she couldn't have been a more supportive, tolerant wife. I hated that one person could have such an overbearing effect on others, that he could make or break a situation with a shift of his mood, and I resented that he possessed that level of control. Yes, I loved him, and yes, I could enjoy having certain types of conversations with him. But he also radiated a dichotomy that was hard to describe, one that provided a sense of safety while also stirring a sense of unrest in me. While my sisters remained anchored to him, choosing to overlook the darker aspect of his personality, I dealt with my conflicting feelings by retreating into a measured amount of distance from him.

I had no idea if my dad felt any inner discord during those years, or if he ever grappled with his disciplinary decisions; because my parents were steeped in their religious beliefs, my dad often fell back on dogma in response to us kids. Though I could talk to my mom about anything, I learned early on to be discerning about the topics I brought to my dad. If he didn't open the subject of a conversation, one that was within his comfort zone, it was simply not a conversation to have.

Shortly after I got married and was contemplating having children, I decided to test the waters of adulthood by approaching my dad with a hot-button topic: religion. (Nothing like taking a dive into a boiling pot wearing a bikini, right?) After all, I was a grown woman, and I thought we should be able to talk on a new level now that I had a husband and was no longer a brooding teen under his roof.

Boy, did I misjudge that one.

What's more, I couldn't have chosen a worse scenario to broach the subject in.

The two of us had decided to take a rare road trip from Atlanta—where Bruce was in pilot training—to North Carolina, where my parents lived at the time. As we sailed down the highway with the wind caressing our faces and a feeling of freedom filling the air, I felt a swirl of courage swell inside me. "You know," I said, taking an uncharacteristic leap, "we're going to be starting a family soon . . . and I don't think I'm playing a full game in the Catholic Church."

Silence.

I rolled my eyes slightly toward him while keeping my head forward—*Don't be intimidated. Stay brave*—then shifted them back again.

"So I think we're going to switch to the Episcopal Church."

Continued silence.

I tentatively turned my head toward him this time and saw shallow breaths begin to escape, coupled with something resembling rage rising in his face. Finally, he eased out a question in a tone that conveyed he was appalled, disappointed, and mortified all at once.

"You're thinking of leaving the Catholic Church?"

I felt my heart speed up but held fast to my backbone as I quickly formulated a reply that would make him feel included in the decision. "Yes," I said, "I'm thinking about it. And I wanted to talk to you about it."

Well, on his end, that was the end of talking about it. In his mind, leaving the Catholic Church meant eternal damnation; there was simply no explanation or reasoning that he would ever tolerate or understand. His face hardened as he stared through the windshield, and I, knowing immediately that I'd made a huge mistake, turned my gaze back to the passing scenery, wishing I was anywhere but in that passenger seat.

For the rest of the trip, I might as well have been a commuter in a freezing car on autopilot for the icy silence he emanated in response. As was his usual way of responding to something that unsettled him, he fell on his defense of shutting me out, and I mentally vowed not to slide into such a biting vortex with him ever again.

I never imagined that in the years to come, after I'd become a mother myself, the man I'd come to fear in some ways and had a difficult time respecting would open my heart to him —in a way I never saw coming.

FOR THE DEFICITS in his parenting and his inadequacy in being emotionally consistent, my dad received the ultimate do-over as each of us began having children of our own. I had expected him to want to pass down his fatherly guidance, holding fast to his strict beliefs on child-rearing and imposing them on us. But instead, he displayed an uncharacteristic softening in the presence of his grandchildren. Like a racecar that had been traveling steadfastly for hundreds of laps, then suddenly spinning out and facing the opposite direction for the duration of the race, he became willing to contribute—in a positive way—to conversations surrounding self-esteem and empowerment of kids, topics he never touched when we were growing up. As one grandchild turned into nine, he became even more animated, creative, and funny, and the part of him that relished encouraging and participating in antics grew too. Once, for example, he and Bruce had a mustache-growing contest. To make it even more fun, he drew mustaches on all three of my sons—something he would have done with us but not in the same gentle way he did with the boys—which they thought was hilarious.

He also engaged each grandchild in similar ways that he did with us, only once again, he wasn't so harsh. He'd gather the kids in the patio around our pool and quiz them. When they didn't know an answer, instead of responding in the disappointed and gruff way he had used with us, he merely teased them gently, in a way I didn't know he had in him. When, on occasion, he'd slip into his old self and point out their weak points in a less-than-encouraging way, one of us adults would intervene and remind him that his manner of teasing wasn't acceptable. Instead of becoming angry or defensive, he'd willingly adjust his behavior, as if he was learning something new and appreciated how it felt.

As I watched him interact with my sons, nieces, and nephews, I was overwhelmed by a single dominant observa-

tion: that if there was a word greater than adoration, that is
what those children felt for my dad.

To say that it warmed my heart to see this stark trans-
formation was undeniably true, but it also brought my unre-
solved issues with my dad to the surface. *Why couldn't he be*
tender like that with all of us, especially Michael? Why did he feel
the need to be so strict and unyielding with his own kids, yet so
easygoing and lighthearted with his grandchildren?

It was something I knew I needed to come to terms with,
if only for my own sense of peace . . . I just didn't know when
or what would surface that would weaken the layers of resentment the prior years had formed into a hardened mass
inside me.

ONE OF THE traits that had blossomed as we kids became
adults was my dad's willingness to be reflective and ask questions he wanted genuine answers to. He had always been a
God-fearing man with tremendous faith, and he had relied on
the doctrines of the church to guide him as a father. But now,
he seemed open to looking at decisions he had made, something that I couldn't help but admire him for.

At some point, he admitted that he had endured abuse in
the Catholic school he attended. It was difficult to reconcile
how he could suffer from his own memories of being beaten at
the hands of church brothers while imposing the same nightmare on his own children. I was grateful I had mostly escaped
his physical punishments, but his actions had created a level of
guilt and imbalance between what felt fair and right among me
and my siblings. Though his admission didn't absolve him
from inflicting on us kids the pain he had suffered, it did touch
my heart with newfound understanding. I felt empathy for

him as a little boy, something I'd never considered before. I reasoned that he was merely a person who repeated negative cycles of child-rearing methods simply because it's what he knew, even though he was aware of what that kind of treatment did to harm him as a child. But the most powerful thing that came from his disclosure was how my love for him suddenly became stronger and more unconditional, and how it awakened even more kindness in me as a mother and a person.

Releasing the burden of the abuse he experienced as a child created a visible shift in my dad, one buoyed by his unshakable faith and that conveyed a willingness to get things right from that point forward. Though he didn't apologize for being so harsh with us, or directly express regret for actions he took as a father, I somehow felt the distance I'd put between us over the years in an act of self-preservation suddenly become a little shorter. The gap wouldn't close in an instant; there was too turbulent a history for that. But I couldn't help but wonder just how much each of us could be softened toward each other if given the right climate.

His door had been opened slightly. I just needed to make sure that mine was open too.

ONE DAY, around 1991, I went over to my dad's with a word-working project. He loved the craft and had an entire area devoted to it in his garage. He was immersed in building a table of some kind, and I planned to work alongside him on whatever it was I was trying to create.

On that particular day, as he was smoothing out the edges of the tabletop, he peered up at me with a sincere look on his face.

"How did you view me growing up?" he asked.

My eyebrows eased upward in surprise. I glanced down and thought for a moment. "In one word?" I asked.

"Yes."

I paused only briefly. "Overwhelmed."

He immediately dropped his head dramatically into his hand, then slowly raised it and stared directly into my eyes. "*Totally,*" he said.

I could almost feel that the exhale accompanying his response carried decades of baggage he'd been dragging around. I also realized that that single word, and the way in which he said it, conveyed that perhaps for the first time as a father, he felt completely heard in a way he probably never had.

IN 1999, my parents were living in North Carolina, and my dad came to Washington DC to see David and me run our first marathon for the Marine Corps. The night before, he took us to dinner in Georgetown, and on the walk back to the hotel afterward, I was holding his arm in the usual way when I noticed his balance was a little off.

"Is everything okay, Dad?" I asked, unaccustomed to seeing him be anything but robust. "Are you dizzy?"

"No," he said, "I'm okay. That happens every so often."

I brushed it off as he seemed to and continued ambling together down the street.

None of us knew it at that time, but my dad was suffering from the early signs of Parkinson's.

Over the next months, Dad's symptoms ranged from tremors—which he thankfully never had too badly—to blank facial expressions, accelerated walking with the inability to stop the momentum, muscle wasting and aching, dementia, and general discomfort. As time passed, it was devastating to witness that this man who was once strong, in control, and capable of so many things was being reduced to a shadow of his former self. Valium controlled some of the symptoms and made him a lot more even-keeled than others with the disease, but it also numbed his personality. As you might imagine, living three thousand miles apart and not seeing each other on a daily or even weekly basis, the new deficits in his physical mobility were notable each time we saw each other.

On one of my parents' visits to California, my dad was noticeably gloomy. At 10:00 a.m., instead of being wide awake and ready for his day, he wanted to rest. As he settled into bed, he patted it and invited me to sit with him.

"You're not feeling like yourself today, are you?" I offered sympathetically.

"No . . . sometimes it's like that lately."

I was used to his seesawing moods, but this was clearly related to his new condition.

"Well, I'll let you rest," I said, getting up to leave.

"No." He reached for my hand. "Don't leave. Stay and talk to me."

I turned to him and smiled. "Okay, then," I said, plopping down on the bed, "what would you like to talk about?"

He thought for a moment. "You know . . . I'm a lucky man to have six attentive kids and your mother as my constant companion."

I patted his hand. "That's sweet of you to say. And yes, I agree!"

We both laughed.

After a brief pause, I said, "Dad . . . are you scared of the end?"

He looked away momentarily. I watched his face for a

sign of how he was going to respond, but he gave nothing away. Finally, in a slow and intentional cadence he said, "You know, I view that as my biggest adventure yet."

I squeezed his hand and nodded knowingly.

Full of faith, and always looking for the next mountain to climb or challenge to conquer—that was the best of my dad.

MY FATHER BRAVED his years with Parkinson's with his usual strength, but it was how he was there for me that perhaps affected me most profoundly.

During Bruce's last year, both my parents sensed that something wasn't right with me. I confided in each of them— separately—that I was finding it increasingly difficult to deal with Bruce's perspective, and that I felt guilty about not being able to maintain my personal happiness and lightheartedness about life. All of it was affecting my feelings for Bruce and I felt terrible.

My mother was a kind listener but, as was typical for her, didn't want to become overly involved and simply offered me platitudes. "Marriage isn't easy." Or "Marriage is work." Or, the topper, "Marriage is a commitment for life, for better and for worse." She was loving and well-intentioned as she delivered her stock answers, but she didn't leave me feeling terribly inspired.

My dad, on the other hand, was particularly attentive to my concerns. In contrast to my mom—and to the way he had been when I was younger—he was willingly supportive and grateful to be confided in, offering me hard-won insight and thought-provoking questions. Oh, how I felt heard! It was as if that day in his garage, when he had asked how I saw him growing up and

I told him honestly, he had internalized that feeling of finally being heard on some level, and he had taken the opportunity to return that understanding to me. He not only took me seriously and empathized in a way that felt like fresh air, but he was practical and wise in his advice, which was exactly what I needed to get me through those trying months.

IN JULY OF that same year, sitting on the patio overlooking the Pacific Ocean, I called Dad on his birthday. During our conversation, my marital unrest came up again.

"Come to North Carolina," he said. "You and Mom and I'll go to Myrtle Beach for a few days. It'll give you a break."

It was an unexpected and genuine offer. I agreed to it and relaxed a little.

He ended our call the same way he always did, by telling me he loved me. Only this time, it wasn't the words that meant so much, but the way he said them—so full of love that it was almost palpable—that stayed with me long after I hung up the phone.

Soon after, I told Bruce about our conversation. I often went to see my parents alone, so I didn't think much of telling him I planned to go to North Carolina without him. But Bruce was in such a bad place at the time that he felt uncharacteristically hurt and betrayed by the invitation, taking the exclusion of him as a snub from the in-laws he'd grown to love and depend on for decades. Although that wasn't my parents' intention, nor mine, in his toxic state of mind that was the only conclusion he could draw.

To avoid hurting him further, though I desperately wanted to go, I decided not to join my parents in Myrtle Beach after all.

꧁

THE FOLLOWING MONTH, in August of 2008, I received a phone call from my mother on my way to the hospital where I was working.

"Mary," she began in her calm way. "Your father's been in a horrible accident." Then she added with a measured breath, "With Michael."

I brought my hand to my mouth. "Oh my God . . . are they . . .?"

"They're both alive," she quickly assured me. Then her toned changed slightly to a more perturbed one. "Michael was driving. They were hit head on going about thirty miles an hour. Your brother's fine. But your father . . . he's unable to move right now."

As a nurse, I immediately took that to mean he was paralyzed, either temporarily or worse. But at the time, my mother didn't have any additional information, so all I could do was wait.

Later that afternoon, Bruce came to tell me in person what the doctors had determined on further post-accident assessment: that my dad would forever be a quadriplegic.

My heart sank as the reality of what that meant settled over me like an ominous cloud: that level of severe immobility would impact every part of his and my mom's lives.

"What are they going to do?" I whispered to no one in particular.

"Your mom said she's going to care for him at home," Bruce said, "because he would want it that way."

I nodded. Of course my mom would continue to stand by him, no matter what. *Marriage is a commitment for life, for better and for worse.*

I immediately flew to North Carolina. During the flight, I went over and over what a proposal of allowing him to die with dignity would sound like, how it was likely the best option for him, and for my mom. It broke my heart to think of my strong, handsome father being even more diminished than the Parkinson's had rendered him, of that stern military man who had softened like a teddy bear with his grandchildren being no longer able to hug them, of the father I'd come to love deeply and could now openly talk to losing the capacity for such a connection. But when I walked into his ICU room, his eyes captured me to my soul. They were so alive and bright with vibrancy that it instantly dimmed any thought I had of interfering with his life.

What also struck me was something that to most might sound unusual, but that with my Catholic upbringing I clearly understood. Being such a devout man who truly believed in the tenets of the Church, my father likely believed he had a penance to pay for the sometimes harsh and harmful choices he'd made as a husband and father—and that his illness and subsequent paralysis was satisfying that penance in a divine way. Knowing how my dad saw life in the reflection of our religion, I took comfort in knowing that he would see this phase at the end of his life being his opportunity to make things right with God—and even see the justice in Michael, the son he had been hardest on, being the cause of the accident. In his mind, for accepting this fate, and having the time to be introspective and ask for forgiveness, he wouldn't be held in purgatory, nor would he be condemned to hell. Whatever suffering he was experiencing was part of his walk with God, and though he could no longer express himself verbally, I fully believe he held space for the distinct possibility that all of it was relevant to the afterlife—and his place in it.

The time I spent with him was relatively short, and I had no idea if it would be the last. All I knew was that when he mouthed the words "I love you" to me as I got up to leave, I would cherish them forever.

December 5, 2008

Mom called yesterday to tell me Dad was failing. His O_2 sats are in the 70s with no way to raise them for any length of time. This is the path it takes, I guess. I want to jump on a plane and do something, but I know there's nothing left for me to do. This is the ending of the ending we've been living since August 9.

I feel numb about another major event occurring in our lives. I've missed my dad so much these past couple weeks . . . he would have been so supportive with Bruce's passing. I actually feel like I can hear his words some days:

"Do you feel like you can handle this? Then move ahead and survive this. I see no reason why you can't be in charge of this situation. Bruce was a great guy, but something snapped. I've seen it happen with so many successful men. My experience has been . . ."

His words would be so comforting, with so much common sense and love . . .

What am I grateful for today?

My dad and all the years of having a father who loved me. A dad I was so proud of as a Marine. He showed me the world. He taught me how to seek out adventures and fall in love with them. He watched

*me handle challenges and was willing to lend a
nonjudgmental ear when needed. He continued to try
in spite of his interpersonal limitations. We all have
them, but he never gave up trying to get past his. He
grew to accept what he had once deemed
unacceptable in his family. He marveled at and
adored his grandkids. He thought the Odgers boys
were incredible young men. He loved watching their
success, and it mattered to him the choices they
made. He liked the way Bruce and I raised them, and
he had so much empathy for their shortcomings . . . I
could see it in his face. I think he knew how much it
took to get through his own, and he could hardly
bear that difficulty for those he loved so much.*

*One of his most lasting legacies is that he was
always interested. Always. He was the epitome of the
lifelong learner, so well read and so willing to share.
He was a skilled master at discussing both sides of a
subject while allowing you to take in the wealth of
knowledge he had cultivated. I'll forever hear him
say, "Talk to me." As a little girl, he'd sometimes
invite me to come upstairs and chat while he
changed out of his uniform. He loved the way I'd lie
on the bed and go on about my day. In spite of his
busy life, he somehow conveyed that he had time for
me. Yes, there were periods when it seemed like he
couldn't be bothered, or times when he froze me out,
but deep down, I always sensed he'd rather be with
us than with people in the outside world . . .*

❦

ONLY FOUR MONTHS after the accident, on December 5, my father slipped away peacefully.

I was never able to tell him Bruce had died.

Later that day, I called each of the boys. Patrick was tender-hearted and tearful; Matt was strong; David was stunned. All three were concerned about me, enveloping me in their love and caring.

Matt came over with his girlfriend and we walked along the beach for a bit. It felt like the perfect place to honor Dad. Though I felt his time had come, I also felt that he had somehow chosen it—that he had willingly freed us from our constant concern and from the 24-hour care he required that weighed so heavily on Mom and his team of caregivers.

My heart ached that my dad was gone, but it was a completely different level of grief from the one I was immersed in with Bruce. It's difficult to describe, but in one way, this grief was layered into the sea of mourning I was already swimming in; in another, it existed separately, as an entity all its own. It was an odd feeling to lose a parent, to have that chapter of my life as my father's daughter close, to no longer have him to talk to, to confide in. But it also brought with it a sense of relief, that the suffering he was going through in the end was over. I was grateful that he'd had such an amazing long life; it was almost palpable how full of love I imagined his spirit self felt, and I smiled as I envisioned how glorious it must have been for his enormously strong faith to have culminated in a meeting with his Creator.

He had told me that he viewed the end as his biggest adventure yet.

I truly felt he was off to enjoy it immensely.

‿

I could have never foreseen that in only eight days, my youngest son, in an act that would take me months to unravel and years to accept and comprehend, would leave this earth to join him.

patrick

*A*FTER THE BIRTHS OF DAVID AND MATTHEW, I HAD envisioned a third child rounding out our family in the most wonderful way. While a part of me wished for the chance to raise a daughter, I couldn't help but imagine that if the baby was another boy, we would have the makings of a near-perfect threesome. And with the arrival of Patrick, I indeed saw my vision come true.

His eldest brother David had come into our lives on March 3, 1982, at just 27 weeks' gestation, weighing only two pounds, seven ounces. It was touch and go in the beginning, but even with the frailness of his too-early debut, he seemed to be filled with the spirit of a giant—of an extraordinary human being who was simply not yet old enough to understand and use his greatness.

As our little fighter grew, we were disheartened to witness that meeting typical developmental milestones was a challenge for him. We chalked it up to his being a preemie, but by the time he reached preschool age, he seemed more suited to a special education program than a traditional preschool, so we enrolled him in an excellent program.

Although he was well liked in his class, David often found social connections with his peers extremely difficult. In my exhaustive search for answers on how to help him progress, I discovered that he displayed what is known in the psychology world as "unoccupied play," where he didn't engage with other children but instead participated in random movements with no objective. At the same time, he demonstrated aspects of "solitary play," where he played alone and chose toys and activities different from those around him, uninterested or unaware of what the other kids were doing.

I learned that both of these activities are important for children, especially between two and three years of age—the period when cognitive, physical, and social skills have not yet fully developed. For David, however, he remained in aspects of these stages until he was seven or eight. He also exhibited a series of repetitive actions, such as beating his chest, rapping his fingertips on his high chair while he waited for his food, and saying the same word or line over and over, such as "Daddy go bye bye." The only diagnoses we were given were ADHD and Tourette's Syndrome, neither of which felt completely accurate. But with nothing else to lean on, we focused on treatments for those. None made much of a difference, though, and as his behaviors progressed, it became clear to me that something was definitely wrong—something that had, in contrast to what the doctors continued to claim, nothing to do with his early arrival.

WHEN DAVID WAS just shy of three, on February 21, 1985, Matthew entered our lives as a physically sturdy baby with blonde curls and the inquisitive blue eyes of his dad and older brother. By the time he was a toddler, unlike his gregarious older brother, he seemed more prone to pondering life than verbalizing it. At times, I actually felt I could see the wheels turning in his head as he tried to make sense of the world.

From as far back as I can remember, people called him an "old soul," and he came to be the one David turned to and admired.

It's not uncommon for children from the same parents to be radically different, but from the start, almost everything was difficult for David, while nearly everything came easily to Matthew; as each boy reached developmental milestones, it became more and more apparent that Matthew picked up on things that David did not. As a result, Matthew instinctively assumed the role of protector, sometimes appearing more like the older sibling. And while the boys loved each other, their stark differences could sometimes be a source of frustration for one another, and I wondered how that would influence their relationship as brothers.

So when Patrick came along in 1987, I was naturally curious—after having two such contrasting children—which of the four of us, if any, he might favor. I was also curious how the balance of our little family would be altered with his presence.

ONCE WE BROUGHT Patrick home, relatively little time seemed to pass before the dynamic of the brothers took shape; by the time Patrick was a mobile member of the family, he became the seeming bridge that gave the threesome its special bond. I know it sounds like an exaggeration (and yes, mothers can be accused of that when it comes to our children), but it truly was as if Patrick was custom ordered and specially made for our family. From the beginning, David and Matthew found common ground in their love for their baby brother. They log-rolled him all over the house, sang to him when he cried, climbed into his crib with "breakfast" (which was once a bag of hot dog buns stolen from the bottom shelf of the pantry), and delighted in looking out for him. For once, the two polar opposite brothers were drawn together as if by a magnetic force, a little squealing, joyful human who in every way made our family feel complete.

By the time Patrick was three, I decided to enroll him in Montessori school so that he would have engagement outside of his brothers in a warm academic environment. Though I believed the few hours a day would benefit him immensely, truth be told, I felt like I was kicking my baby out a bit early—not so unlike my paternal grandmother had done with my father—but I didn't have to feel that way for long.

Upon arrival that first morning, I videotaped Patrick getting out of the big blue Suburban, dressed in his little striped shorts and brand new shoes, with his Mickey Mouse lunch box in hand—not a typical square lunch box with Mickey's face on it, but an actual plastic replica of Mickey's head. I thought it was hilarious and Patrick took to it like a new friend. Standing there so cute on the sidewalk, he waved as I turned briefly away to film the sign that read "Montessori Children's House" in front of the school. When I turned around, Patrick was gone. I immediately looked in all the obvious places: the car, up and down the street, among the sparse group of other children starting their first day. But no Patrick. Frantic, I ran toward the entrance, my eyes darting for any sign of my son when I caught a familiar sight: Mickey smiling at me. He was sitting on the shelf inside the door where all the lunches were deposited on arrival. Feeling momentary relief, I quickly scanned the foyer, and just inside to the left sat Patrick, on the "tape line" intended for the little ones. In the short time I had dashed around looking for him, he had found the room on his own, taken a seat in his designated spot, and become a captive audience for lovely Miss Linda J. and Mrs. Via G., who soon became the teacher of his dreams.

As a mother, I had imagined comforting my little boy as he cried when I left him, or acted nervous in his new environment. But instead, I found myself wishing he would comfort *me*, the mother he didn't seem to need when he was barely out of diapers. As his teachers were having to console most of the children on their first day, Patrick was already self-reliantly on his own, front and center, ready for class to begin. That snapshot of him sitting where he'd been instructed, with no fuss or fear emanating from him, was a telling preview of how my youngest child would tackle life from then on: quietly confident with a streak of hardwired independence.

With Patrick now old enough to hold a conversation, the banter between him and his brothers was endless, free, and moved through our world like the pulse of a sustaining life force. Matthew, who had the dexterity for sports, started playing soccer by age five, and Patrick followed only a few years behind. But David struggled with anything that required visual processing and spatial relations. This not only left out sports, but we eventually discovered that it made it impossible to calculate math problems, judge distances while riding his bike, learn karate, or do something as simple as tie his shoes. Intellectually, he seemed to get it, but physically these tasks simply didn't translate. It seemed little time passed before I was shuttling Matthew and Patrick to practices, games, school activities, or various friends' houses. But David tended to prefer more solitary pursuits. So, to provide him with the same opportunities for interaction that his brothers had, Bruce and I worked hard to integrate David into activities such as Cub Scouts and music lessons, neither of which particularly sparked his interest, but gave him a schedule of activities like his brothers as well as a sense of belonging.

While multiple skills may have eluded David, being immersed in books provided endless fascination for him. His greatest passion became reading, and he read everything he could get his hands on. It was such a relief and a gift to know that books provided a happy space for him, and that they gave him a portal to "keep up with" his more active and academically inclined brothers. Though there were times he displayed jealousy in not joining Matthew in some activity, for the most part, he never appeared irritated by his unconventional development; he merely resided in his comfort zone while his brothers resided in theirs. His inability to connect with others did, however, limit his friendships with other children and left him isolated from invitations for play dates and birthday parties. While our hearts ached for him, we made sure he had all the therapies, coaching, and tutoring available to help him thrive, and we constantly strove to ensure he flourished in an abundant river of love and encouragement.

Although David's limitations proved frustrating at times, Bruce and I—along with compassionate grandparents, aunts, uncles, and cousins—managed to give him a life that accommodated his special learning needs. Perhaps one of our greatest assets, though, was Patrick. For years, trying to at once uphold David's self-esteem while not holding Matthew back, simply because his brother couldn't partake in the same activities, was akin to riding a teeter-totter I could rarely get off. But Patrick was like a stabilizer who fit snugly between his brothers, balancing the seesaw with his inherent gift of meeting them halfway. It was almost as if David and Matthew wobbled on a two-wheel bike, but Patrick created a welcome tricycle that took an appreciable amount of the unsteadiness away.

Patrick also possessed an uncanny understanding of his eldest brother. Matthew certainly supported, included, and was a role model for David, but the six years between David and

Patrick afforded particular liberties, one of which was humor. Though Matthew's friends were all understanding of David's eccentricities, Patrick's way of poking fun at them—and not focusing on his differences—made David laugh. With a special brand of directness without ever being demeaning, Patrick made David feel at ease with his quirks, and that consistent air of humor soothed the sibling tension that sometimes hovered within our house of growing boys. It also contributed to David having a safe space of sorts to just be himself.

From the outside, it appeared we were living a perfect life, in our dream home with our boys—and in many ways we were. Yes, we had our share of difficulties, but to me our family felt perfect in its flaws, like a well-worn but warm winter coat or an aged piece of furniture that becomes more beautiful with time.

FOR ALL THE joy our three sons brought to our lives, David's constant roadblocks were undeniably hard on Bruce's and my marriage. David's weak points affected us each differently, though, which somehow gave us the strength to buoy each other when one of us was down. But for Bruce it was something deeper than simply the realization that our firstborn wouldn't have the kind of life we hoped he would have.

During a marriage counseling session, Bruce admitted he harbored anger toward me for giving birth prematurely. The therapist, trying to remain neutral, was clearly shocked by his confession. When she turned to read my reaction, she expected to see me destroyed by having my husband blame me for something I had no control over. But instead, after years of not knowing what was going on in his head, I was relieved to hear his honest words. I, myself, had suffered for years with horrible guilt from what felt like having failed my child, that if I'd been "better" at childbearing, I would have given David the same chance in the world that his brothers received. When Bruce held a mirror to those feelings, it gave me the opportunity to apologize to Bruce—and to myself—even though it was for something that wasn't my fault. Simply being able to relate to Bruce allowed us to communicate in a way we'd never been able to before, and his truth gave me the chance to comfort, reassure, and empathize with him, while I did the same for myself.

For me, my relief in having shared this burden with Bruce was a turning point of sorts in our marriage and as parents. He was still naturally resistant to opening up when something didn't sit right with him, but I did feel closer to him after that episode—and the open conversation we'd shared gave me an added dose of hope of what the future would hold for us.

And until 2008, that hope rarely faltered.

IN 2002, Patrick started high school where Matthew was already established as an immensely popular senior. As he always had, Patrick looked up to his brother. In a certain way, he had relished being in Matthew's shadow, striving to be like him, yet drawing a healthy line between them when something didn't resonate. In other words, Patrick emulated his brother only so far as Matthew's path aligned with his; if Patrick wanted to go in a different direction—such as when he didn't want to join Cub Scouts while Matthew was devoted to it—he made his preference known. But there was no doubt that Matthew, with his instinctive leadership skills that magnetized people to him and his innate wisdom and compassion that won him scores of friends, was the ideal big brother.

Being one of the captains of the football team was yet another perk: Matthew took freshman Patrick under his wing and gave him an automatic "in" with the crowd of upperclassmen. It seemed that Patrick, with his own streak of confidence, couldn't be bolstered any higher, or been more proud of being the brother of one of the most admired guys on the high school campus.

AS PATRICK'S FIRST year of high school came to an end, so too did Matthew's senior year. As we had with David, we hosted a pre-graduation ceremony meal with all the cousins, extended family, and best friends, and there was no shortage of funny and sentimental toasting of the graduate.

Throughout the festivities, though he exuded his signature sensitivity and adoration of his brother, I watched Patrick remain quiet, struggling for composure and on the brink of tears. Later that afternoon, while I was ironing Matt's gown to wear that evening, Patrick came into my room. I immediately set the iron down, sensing he wanted to talk.

"I was too afraid of crying to give Matt a toast," he admitted, his eyes welling with tears. "I knew I'd lose it in front of everyone if I told them how proud I was of my brother."

I felt my heart nearly burst with all the love I knew Patrick felt for Matthew.

"Well, you don't have to miss the opportunity to tell him how you feel," I said. "Write him a letter. You have time. Do it now."

Without missing a beat, Patrick left to grab paper and a pen, then returned and wrote the letter right there in our master bathroom, pouring his gentle, emotional heart out like a powerful river of love that couldn't be stopped.

6/18/03

Matt,

I knew I wasn't going to be able to make a toast for you at dinner tonight. I didn't think I could do it without crying. From when we were all little to now, you have always been a hero to me. You have always taught me right from wrong and what to do and not do. I have always looked up to you. I remember at every football game they would call your name as a captain. I've always dreaded the day you have to leave for college and the day is getting closer and closer. I won't be able to see you at school anymore or talk to you late at night. I've always been proud that you are my brother. Usually people feel scared becoming a freshman, but I knew I was safe because you were there. I know you will achieve all the goals you set at Purdue. I'm very proud of you. Good Luck!

Love,

Patrick Odgers

As a toddler, Patrick had expressed inexplicable fears of things like kitty cats, fire engines, and burglars, and he had often been plagued as a child with bad dreams. But he wasn't that scared little boy anymore. Perhaps having that year under Matthew's protective arm had been the catalyst for his growing up and overcoming those childhood fears. But as I read the sweet words Patrick wrote to his brother, I smiled knowing that one thing hadn't changed: Patrick's deep sensitivity.

I always saw it as an admirable trait.

I didn't know how profoundly it affected how my son lived his life.

AS THE YEARS continued to pass, the boys' white-blond hair turned to brown, the crystal blue eyes David and Matthew received from their father slowly changed to green like mine, and they all towered over me at 6'2". But despite the similar coloring and size, each had his own distinctive look. They also had their own brand of fun with each other—but Patrick had a particular flair for the comical.

At age fourteen, David had finally received a diagnosis for his behaviors that made sense: Asperger's syndrome, a form of autism characterized by higher than average intellectual ability, but certain disruptive social skills and repetitive patterns of interests and abilities. While David's IQ was on the lower end from having been born premature, the diagnosis otherwise fit him to a tee. Having an explanation for David's unique outlook on the world was a relief to all of us, but perhaps especially to David, who had never fully understood why he was labeled "different" by other kids. But now, when someone responded negatively to one of his quirks or unexpected retorts, he would simply tell them he couldn't help it because he was autistic. Over time, however, he used what we jokingly called his "autism excuse" to excess; almost every unacceptable action he took or comment he made, he blamed on his autism.

As a mother, I would have gentle conversations with him

about him using Asperger's as a crutch, that he had more control over certain behaviors than he was copping to. But Patrick would flat-out call him out on it.

"Give me a break," he might say. "That's a lame excuse and you know it." Or, "Really, David? Like we've never heard that one before."

His lighthearted comments would diffuse the uncomfortable scene and David would usually break into laughter. Patrick seemed to be the only one who could get away with his blunt manner of teasing David, which David always knew had brotherly love underneath.

But Patrick's ribbing didn't stop there.

Because David's visual limitations kept him from driving, everyone took turns taking him to and from work, the movies, or friends' houses. Once Patrick got his license, being the loyal little brother (and perhaps foreseeing opportunities to pull a few pranks), he was no exception.

One night, Patrick and his best friend Cody agreed to pick David up from work at Costco. As David exited the building into the dark and empty parking lot, he saw only one car: his brother's. The bass was blaring, vibrating the pavement, and inside were two guys dressed up like a couple of thugs with kerchiefs around their faces. Wondering if his brother had been carjacked, or possibly taken hostage, David tentatively approached, trembling and fearful of the worst. When he reached the car, Patrick and Cody pulled down the kerchiefs and erupted in laughter. I imagine David wanted to pummel them both, but instead he cracked up right along with them.

Another classic Patrick stunt that involved David happened when he picked his brother up from work one night and was accosted by the putrid smell of David's shoes. I had been meaning to get him a new pair but kept forgetting. Patrick, however, was too revolted to look—or rather breathe—in the opposite direction. On the way home, he insisted on stopping at a shoe store to buy David a new pair.

When David came through the door, he waltzed into the kitchen in a particularly jovial mood, making kicking strides like a kid. "Look at my new shoes Patrick bought me," he beamed.

Just then, Patrick sailed past me and under his breath said, "You owe me eighty bucks."

Later that night, in conversation during dinner, the boys confessed between bouts of hysterics that they had chucked the old pair out the window on the Poway Grade. For weeks afterward, every time we drove down that highway, one of those awful shoes was sitting on the dividing yellow line. The sight of it never ceased to bring howling laughter from us all.

BY 2008, David had become a young man with a steady job living at The Independence Center in Culver City, California; Matthew had graduated from Purdue, finished a year of teaching English in South Korea, and was now awaiting law school; and Patrick had followed in his brother's footsteps and was now a sophomore at Purdue. We had all moved forward in our own ways after losing our house to the fire, and Patrick—despite being away at college—had stayed with his high school girlfriend, a lovely girl named Danielle.

A year older than Patrick, Danielle was determined, focused, and had concrete plans for her future—which motivated Patrick to keep in stride with her, a path that seemed to suit him perfectly. Though she was attending nursing school in California, putting two thousand miles between them, Patrick's college roommate, Grant, joked that Patrick acted like a married man on campus. I was concerned that he was too young to take their relationship to that level, but I couldn't help but admire Patrick's devotion to her and to the solid direction they were headed toward together.

At the end of Patrick's spring semester, I flew to Indiana to pick him up from college. Some months before, I had proposed that we take a trip, just the two of us, to Paris and Prague for some "stolen mother/son time," and Patrick had enthusiastically agreed. I hadn't known if he'd be willing to spend time away from Danielle, so when he said yes, I was over the moon.

On the way to the airport, Patrick asked to make a pit stop. As he walked back to the car, he had an odd smile on his face, like something had struck him funny but with some degree of discomfort.

After settling back into the passenger seat, he shifted uncomfortably. "I have something to tell you," he said.

Danielle had just spent a short vacation with him, and I felt certain it had to do with her. A tingling flush traveled up my chest to my throat as I waited for him to gather what seemed to be courage.

But instead of words leaving his mouth, Patrick slowly lifted his shirt. From his armpit to his hip was our hometown—San Diego—tattooed in multicolored ink.

My mouth dropped open. I had feared he was going to confess he had proposed to Danielle, but this was the materialization of another fear altogether: that my sons would succumb to the tattoo frenzy prevalent among the youth population.

"Oh, Patrick," I sighed, my voice dripping with disappointment. "Why would you do that?"

We argued. I felt betrayed as a mother who had begged her boys not to submit to something so impulsive and lasting.

While I admired that Patrick had a mind of his own, I also cringed at the thought of him making decisions that could affect him—good or bad—for the rest of his life.

After a pocket of silence, I threw the mother dagger. "Did you even think of me?"

Patrick pulled back as if I'd slapped him across the face. The uncertain smile he'd been sporting morphed into an open-lipped, wordless grimace.

"Mom," he said with sorrow in his voice, "please don't say that."

But I knew in my heart that if his mind had gone toward me even once while making the decision, he would have never gone through with it. This was the teen who would sit next to me on the couch, on or an airplane, and hold one of my hands or bend my fingers back one at a time, mischievously waiting for me to wince, never self-conscious about us being close. Yet here he was, an apparent master at compartmentalizing, pushing anything that might conflict with his desires into a proverbial box where it couldn't enter his psyche and foil his plans.

I was suddenly flooded with thoughts of how, throughout the years, I had found myself perplexed by my youngest son. At times, he did things that mystified me, things I didn't see coming. David and Matthew had typically been overt with their intentions and actions, but Patrick had always possessed the ability to shock me. It had never been life-shattering, but it had unhinged me at times nonetheless. I suppose I wanted the safety of his being relatively predictable—not just in the consistent ways he showed affection toward me, his dad, or his brothers, or how our closeness had never waned since he was a baby—but in the way he conducted his entire life, which I knew deep down was a pipe dream that would only leave me disappointed.

The truth was that once Patrick made up his mind about something he felt strongly about, nothing and no one could sway him. Even as a toddler, he had no qualms about stating what he wanted. My father once teased him at the end of a visit, saying, "David and Matthew are going home with your mom and dad, but you're going to spend the night here with Grama and me." Patrick became still and serious. "No, Grampa. Tonight I'm going home with my mom."

My dad simply looked at me and shook his head. "That boy knows exactly what he wants."

It wasn't that Patrick was strong-headed and stubborn. It was more that his sensitive nature was such that any outside discouragement would weigh on him and potentially shift his trajectory. This was why he avoided conflicting opinions about something he wanted to do—which was why he had pushed me completely out of his mind when he decided to get the tattoo. But that was Patrick. To avoid the possibility of feeling bad, or of having someone upend an idea he had, he instead often chose not to consider the potential reaction of others to some of his decisions. If he had, he may have been less likely to do some of the things he did.

This tunneled, spontaneous thinking, coupled with how deeply he felt every human emotion, was what would lead my beautiful boy to ultimately do something unthinkable, something from which there would be no going back.

❦

DESPITE THE RUFFLED start, Patrick and I relished our trip to Europe together. But only five months after we returned, I had the inconceivable task of delivering the news to him in person at Purdue that his father had taken his own life. He shook tearfully in my arms as he sobbed, unable to process that the father he loved with all his heart was gone. Grant, who loved Patrick like a brother, cried quietly for him in the corner. His brothers were with me, and we all felt the stark realization that after years of it being the five of us, we were now a family of four.

Patrick came home for Bruce's funeral, then returned to school shortly afterward. I was concerned that it was too soon, but was comforted that he would be back for Thanksgiving break only a few weeks later. But when Thanksgiving arrived, it seemed Patrick had barely unpacked his bag when he had to turn around and go back to Purdue. Though we had gone to my sister's and I'd helped prepare the festive meal, it seemed we were all trying hard to feign enthusiasm, eating as if we were going through the motions. In the prior three weeks, I had had to force myself to eat to stay strong for those who saw me physically diminishing. I could sense that Patrick felt awkward about leaving me, but I assured him that I would take care of myself, and he was comforted that Danielle would be with me off and on.

At the airport, I got out of the car at the curb, not to help Patrick with his luggage but just to hug him one last time. My head was empty from thinking and grieving so much, but I was never short on words of love and comfort for my sons.

"I love you so much," I said, pressing a letter into Patrick's hand. "Save this for the plane."

He nodded and hugged me tightly. "I love you too, Mom."

Then he pulled away and disappeared into the terminal, turning around for a brief wave, then evaporating into the crowd.

In the letter, now in some box somewhere among what is left of our old life, I told him how proud I was of him, how brave I believed he was. I told him not to worry about his grades, that going back to school was positive motion and would help him heal. I promised that if he wasn't comfortable, I would come to him, or I would buy him a return ticket immediately so that he could come home.

He never asked for either.

DURING THE BRIEF time Patrick was home for that first holiday without his dad, Danielle encouraged him to start a journal. Sometimes I felt she was my alter ego, suggesting the ideas I left unspoken as I tried to be respectful of Patrick's space. Though I worried that she was a little too controlling at times, to be honest, I worried the same about myself. The thing was, someone needed to take control within our out-of-control life, and Danielle did so in a way that felt appropriate; what I didn't say to my nearly grown son, she did. Lucky for me, he welcomed her suggestion of writing as a way to process all the emotion that engulfed him.

I had no idea at the time just how much it would mean.

IN THE DAYS after Patrick returned to school, he called often just to talk. I had only felt comfortable with his return to Purdue because of the support system I knew he had there: Grant and his parents, his new set of friends, and the grief support group on campus. But the loss of Bruce hit him undeniably hard. During each conversation, he would collapse into tears over how much he missed his dad, while I gathered every ounce of strength I had to assure him we would get through the grief and pain together. Then, not one week later, on December 5, I was faced with delivering yet another shocking blow to my son: that his Grampa David had passed away. I heard his voice crack, then he cried as if his broken heart was shattering beyond repair.

LATER THAT WEEK, Patrick called with surprising energy in his voice to tell me he was taking a business class to learn how to help get our family's financial situation—which had been dropped into my lap after Bruce's death—in order. As much as I needed to educate myself and find my way through that part of our life, my heart swelled with love and connection to my son, who wanted desperately to support the family. Bruce had always been completely in charge of our finances and Patrick knew it. I suppose he felt the need to step in for his dad and make things right—an offer that not only touched me but sparked an idea.

"You can be my business partner," I said with sudden enthusiasm.

"Okay, Mom," he agreed. "Sounds good."

"I really need you boys," I added, immediately hoping I hadn't put too much pressure on him by saying so.

"I know," he said. But he didn't sound burdened when he said it. If was more as if he was telling me that he was happy to step up and help, that it was something he truly wanted to do to support me.

We didn't discuss the particulars, but the notion of having Patrick by my side in this way injected me with a much-needed dose of promise—and, I hoped, a sense of optimism for the future for Patrick as well.

"I'm so glad you'll be home for your birthday," I said. "You'll have to let me know what you'd like to do."

Patrick was turning twenty-one on the eighteenth, which was only eight days away. I knew a big part of that celebration would be with his friends, but I still looked forward to throwing him a party at home with his brothers.

"I will," he said. "But please don't worry about doing anything big."

ON FRIDAY NIGHT, December 12, I lay in bed overlooking the ocean. I was trying to read but had a hard time concentrating. Though my sons' voices gave me much-needed comfort, I'd begun to sense it was better not to call at times like this. There wasn't much besides the obvious to discuss, and the underlying thread of our conversations was me silently asking them to help me feel better.

Despite that, I had an overwhelming urge to call Patrick. I picked up the phone but immediately changed my mind. He'd had enough tragic news of late, and though I missed him terribly, I hoped he might have allowed himself to be out having a good time. Plus, when he became a college freshman, he had established a pattern of being unavailable when Bruce or I called on Friday nights or weekends. We sort of laughed it off at first, but Patrick had held fast to his "rules." I actually admired how he was true to to himself in that way, and I loved how he called every Sunday night without fail to check in.

As I gazed out at the moonlit water, I physically ached over the loss of Bruce. I was also deeply worried about how my sons were each coping. Haunted by thoughts and images of how Bruce had left us, I closed my eyes and eventually fell into a fitful sleep.

When I awoke at dawn, it was a gloomy, overcast day peppered with rain. I didn't care, though. I yearned to get outdoors among the trees and walk, so after writing in my journal, I went with Maripat to beautiful Deer Park. There, we stumbled upon the Vietnamese Zen Buddhist monastery where spiritual teacher Thich Nhat Hanh held retreats. As I stood in front of the huge altar, with an enormous statue of Buddha smiling over me, I marveled at the serenity all around me. Lingering raindrops fell gently to the ground from tree limbs; quiet seemed to shield me from the pain of the outside world. Normally, I would be wholly inspired by a slice of heaven like this, but I couldn't feel much of anything on a soul level. *Is this what grief does?* I wondered. *Blot out the senses even in a place as peaceful as this?* On any other day, the smell of the forest would have been intoxicating. But on this day, there was a block I couldn't explain, a weight inside that felt insurmountable. I couldn't understand why I felt so agitated and couldn't fully connect with the peace of it all, but I guessed it was simply how life was for me now.

Shortly after our hike, while we were having breakfast at a restaurant nearby, Maripat's phone rang.

"Mrs. Lloyd," I heard Matthew say tearfully. "Bring my mom home right away."

"Okay, Matt," she said. "We're on our way right now."

It was typical of Maripat to not ask questions. She knew Matthew had had a horribly tough week. He had never been overly willing to share his emotions, but that week, he had broken down on several occasions. I imagined this was the final crack and that he was begging for help. Within seconds, we had paid the bill and were running toward the parking lot.

The minute and a half it took for Maripat and me to get to the car turned out to be the last segment of true peace I would ever have. I must have known it instinctively because I slammed the keys into Maripat's hand and said, "You drive."

Sliding into the passenger seat, I grabbed my phone, which I had left in the car. My heart immediately plummeted when I saw that I had numerous missed calls from Danielle and Grant. In my mind, that could only mean one thing: something was wrong with Patrick.

I dialed Danielle's number. No answer.

"Hurry, drive home," I implored Maripat. "Oh God, hurry."

I grabbed my phone again and called Grant. He picked up right away.

"Mary," he answered between sobs, his emotion raising a fear in me that was akin to someone holding a pillow hard against my face, attempting to suffocate me. "I had to . . . break into his room and I . . . found him . . . hanging."

My world screeched to a halt. I threw my phone onto the floor of the car like a child, as if hurling it away from me would erase the words I just heard. But the adult in me couldn't unhear it, couldn't undo it.

"Patrick's dead," I screamed. "Patrick's dead!" I rocked back and forth, my crossed arms squeezing my ribs like a python, my fists so tight my nails pressed quarter moons into my hands, willing it not to be true.

But it was true.

My sweet Patrick had hanged himself and I couldn't fathom why.

※

IN THE DAYS that followed, to say that I was a shadow of myself would be an understatement. The truth was, I felt completely separate from the world. I was grateful to no longer believe in the vengeful God of my Catholic upbringing, but I couldn't fathom how I, as one person, could be expected to endure such a bombardment of loss. First our home a year prior, then Bruce, then Dad, then . . . Patrick? Up until then, I at times could see the possibility of feeling peace with all the tragedy that had befallen us. I had finally come to terms, for the most part, with losing nearly every material thing and treasure I had possessed in the fire. Dad's passing was fairly expected, and with his profound disability, I actually felt relief in his leaving because his suffering was over. Even Bruce, whose death was like being blindsided by an intruder in the dark, made a degree of sense when I considered his escalating depression and irrational state of mind. I was reeling—and would be for a long time—over losing my husband, but my son? I had suddenly stepped into a new realm of being, one that felt impossible to traverse. How could I survive the death of my Patrick? Nothing about his apparent suicide made even the slightest bit of sense to me.

I knew there would be no rationale to come and rescue me, nothing that would bring my son back. But the mind can be brutal. In place of even a single comforting thought as I tried to understand what could have led my son to this irrevocable choice, thoughts flew at me like arrows I barely had the strength to dodge.

> *Why hadn't I called him that night the way I wanted to? If I had, maybe I could have said something or done something that could have changed his mind.*

> *Why hadn't I realized as a mother that the block I felt at the monastery was a sign? That I couldn't feel peace because something was wrong with Patrick?*

> *Why hadn't I made the trip to Indiana after Dad died? I knew Patrick was shaken to his core over losing his dad, then his grampa. We all were but Patrick, being so sensitive, seemed to take it harder than anyone. I wanted to be with him, but I just didn't have the strength for another trip to*

Purdue . . . and I thought it best to remain with David and Matthew. I was tormented by that decision. Whose suffering should I support? Which child needs me more? It felt like an impossible decision for a mother to make. Maybe I took the path of least resistance in staying in San Diego. I know I went with my gut feeling. But what if my gut was wrong? What if my decision not to go to him had an influence on Patrick's state of mind that night?

As any parent would be, I was accosted by every way I could have possibly saved my son. With Bruce, and now with Patrick, I kept envisioning that I played a key role in the events of their lives, that I could have manipulated them to change the outcome . . . that I mattered that much, had that much power.

But after hearing the details of Patrick's death, and eventually seeing the scene for myself, I came to believe that perhaps the power I thought I possessed in our little fivesome had been nothing more than an illusion. I also came to believe with every fiber of my being what Patrick's true intentions were on that unimaginable night.

AS I HAD lain in bed that Friday night, unable to stay focused on reading and longing to talk to Patrick, he had gone to a party with Grant and some other friends. Danielle wasn't fond of college partying, so Patrick had made it a habit of abstaining for her sake. But on that night, perhaps wanting desperately to have some time out of his grieving mind, he had agreed to go.

Growing up with a certain amount of unpredictability because of my father's relationship with alcohol, I had always feared that my boys would be sucked into drinking and develop the same addiction my dad had. And when Patrick was a teen, my fears became heightened. Patrick didn't become a funny drunk, or even a mean drunk. He became a completely different person—one who was capable of doing deplorable things. After open discussions about what a bad idea it was for him to drink, it clicked for him and he agreed to stop. But Grant admitted to me that he'd seen Patrick down six beers at the party, maybe eight. Grant knew Patrick was in a lot of pain over losing his dad and grandfather, so he just cautiously observed—not realizing he was seeing evidence of Patrick's life taking a turn for the worse.

Shortly before midnight, the group returned to the house they shared and hung out in their central living room for a bit. Around 12:30, Patrick said good-night to everyone and went into his room.

His heavy winter coat was found on the floor, next to a copy of the school newspaper. On the front page was a picture of a fellow student who had jumped from a top-floor window the week before. Patrick had told me about the boy, and had actually asked if he could buy some books about suicide on my credit card at the Purdue campus bookstore. We were both shocked that a young student would do such a thing.

I envision that after he slipped off his coat, he sat on the floor to read the article once again. Being an intensely curious person, I imagine that in his intoxicated state, the article prompted him to fully understand how his father must have felt on the night he killed himself, and an idea came to him that would allow him to be inside his dad's mind when he made that fateful decision.

Using the bathroom counter as a desk—the same way he did on Matthew's graduation day when he poured out his heart to his brother in writing—Patrick wrote a long letter, detailing his sadness yet also remaining upbeat, sharing his feelings in his typical way. His handwriting was not as tidy and controlled as it usually was, but I believed that was due to the alcohol. He left the letter there, along with the blue pen he used to write it. The average person would see it as a typical suicide note, but when I read his words, they didn't feel to me like he was actually saying goodbye. Yes, he wrote about missing his dad and grampa, and he even shared how he loved and appreciated me, but it wasn't a letter that said he was done with his life. As close as he could, I believe he was replicating what a person in a state of hopelessness would write, simply to feel what those words might look like on paper. Bruce had left a brief suicide note; Patrick's was a long and thoughtful letter, open about his emotions at the time but not fatalistic.

Next to the letter, he placed a sharp, fold-up knife. Bruce had employed a similar knife, so Patrick would have wanted the same item his father used to be present. The knife remained unused, which was a clue to me that it was merely a prop in his staged scenario, with no intention of utilizing it to do any harm to himself.

But Bruce had chosen to take his life with double impact.

Patrick had draped and fastened a belt over his pull-up bar. He hadn't intended to actually kill himself, only to get as close as he could to understand how his dad could have inflicted such a brutal act on himself. But in reenacting this horrific scene, I believe he let it go too far to pull out before it was too late. Whether he fell into a brief, drunken sleep, or something else occurred that we'll never fully know, the weight of Patrick's body put pressure on his carotid arteries, cutting off his blood supply and consciousness.

His curiosity, however morbid, had led him to death's door.

The fact that he never meant to walk through it would haunt me forever.

༄

WHILE MY INSTINCT was to go to my son, there was no reason to fly to Indiana. Patrick was gone, and there was nothing as his mother I could do. But my son was 2,000 miles away, and I was desperate to bring him home. In the shadowy state of mind I was floating in, I had no idea how to handle the logistics. I vaguely recall Grant's parents, Becky and Phil, telling me not to worry, that they would help arrange Patrick's transport to California. And by the grace of God and their limitless kindness, they coordinated the police with the funeral home we had just worked with for Bruce to bring my son back to me.

I remember very little of the days that followed. But on December 18, what would have been Patrick's twenty-first birthday, I received a call that his body had arrived.

Surrounded by my entire family—including my mom, who flew out despite having just lost my dad—we were led into the room where Patrick's coffin sat eerily in the center. We all held hands and said a prayer, and then I approached the open casket.

Only weeks ago, when Bruce had died, I had struggled with whether or not to see him.

"You should," Maripat said. "If you do, you may be startled . . . and maybe even have a haunting memory from it. But if you don't, you may always regret it . . . you may never get the closure you need."

I had heeded her advice and braved the viewing. And yes, it did haunt me to see his face, but it gave me a sense of closure as well. I wasn't sure what I really needed at the time, but I knew instinctively that I'd done the right thing.

Now, with Patrick, I was facing the same shock, the same effects, but it was a whole different level of pain. When I saw his precious face, all I could manage in a tortured voice was, "What did you do?" Tears streamed down my cheeks as everyone comforted me. After a brief time, we returned to the salon out front to make the funeral plans.

Needing some air, I was stepping outside when a woman came toward the door. I held it for her, and she stopped.

"Do we know each other?" she asked.

I didn't recognize her, and normally I would have just said no and continued walking. But there was something tender about this woman, something that seemed to connect with me.

"I don't think so," I said.

She shook her head. "Are you sure? Maybe from Del Mar?"

We had only lived there a short time at that point, and I told her so. But even though she couldn't place me, she didn't want to disconnect from me. It was obvious I was distraught with grief, and she wanted to offer comfort.

It turned out that she was a minister as well as a clairvoyant, and after introducing herself to the family as Florence, she turned to me.

"Have you touched him?" she gently asked.

I was taken aback. She didn't know who I'd lost, yet her intuition had told her it was a male.

"No," I said. "I don't know if I can."

"You should," Florence said, rubbing my arm like a dear friend. "It's important for you."

I nodded and allowed her to kindly escort me back into Patrick's room, where his hands were resting on his chest. She gingerly unclasped them and motioned me forward.

"Hold his hands," she said softly.

She stepped back as I took my son's cold, lifeless hands in mine, the hands that had lovingly held mine so many times throughout the years. Though I knew there was no life in him, it was powerful to connect with him physically one more time, something I didn't realize how much I needed until I stood there sobbing over him.

Florence told me that she felt an incredibly strong bond of love between us, that the pull of love was so much stronger than anything he'd left behind. "Tell him you accept his choice," she said softly. "Tell him you just want to understand and that he's the only one who can help you do that."

I nodded and whispered the words to him—but telling him I accepted his decision was more a hopeful attempt at a mindset that might become a reality at some point than something I truly felt.

As I stood there holding Patrick's hand, I imagined he was happy being with his dad and Grampa David. But I knew there was no way he couldn't miss me. Our bond in life had been too great. I wanted us to be a family again, to be together the following week for Christmas. I wanted Bruce to shop for the boys the way he always did, for Patrick to tolerate going to mass and sneak sips of wine at dinner and throw his arms around me because he was so excited about his gifts. I wanted him to beg me to go to Danielle's and to erupt in an enormous smile when I gave in.

I wanted this all to be a nightmare I would wake up from, grateful that none of the pain was true.

At some point, I released Patrick's hands and reached up to touch his hair. He had loved when I scratched his head, the way a person would a puppy. He'd worn his hair gelled for so long that I'd forgotten how soft it could be. As I stroked it, I understood why this woman had appeared like an angel and led me to this moment.

Had I buried my child without having the courage—and the gift—to touch him one last time, to gently tousle his hair the way he had always relished, I'm certain I would have regretted it for the rest of my life.

ON THE DAY of Patrick's funeral, Becky told me that a lot of Patrick's friends had flown out from Indiana, and that she thought it would be a good idea to let them see Patrick privately. Right away, I imagined a bunch of gawkers and said no, but she assured me it wouldn't be like that—that it would help relieve the trauma they were suffering and hopefully bring them closure. So I arranged for only his college friends to see him, and they each expressed how much they appreciated having a last quiet moment with their friend. These kids ended up being a tremendous comfort to me, and it allowed me to connect with Patrick on a whole other level. These were his new people, the ones he chose to spend his time with, have fun with, be there for when they needed him. And now, it was as if Patrick had inspired them to come and be there for me, in a way he knew he never could again.

A FEW WEEKS after Patrick's funeral, Matthew and I made the painstaking trip to Indiana to retrieve Patrick's belongings. One of the most difficult parts of grieving him was having very little of his to hold. Because we'd lost all of our tangible history in the fire, and because Patrick had been away at school, everything he cared about had been toted to college with him, and at home there was no longer a bedroom that was his for me to grieve in.

While I feared how it would affect me to see all of Patrick's things the way he left them, I also felt a sense of purpose in re-entering his space. I was beginning to suspect that there may have been more to his suicide than we initially knew, and I wondered if there was something going on with Patrick I didn't know about, some "dark secret" that might have driven him to do such a horrendous thing.

It was barely above zero in West Lafayette. Warmly bundled and with Matthew by my side, I felt oddly calm. But when I opened the door to Patrick's bedroom, I immediately flinched. The bathroom doorway, where the chin-up bar had been, faced me like a thief who had stolen my son from me. I had told Grant I didn't want anything in Patrick's room touched, so to see that the bar had been removed—even to spare me the sight of it—unnerved me. But as I glanced around, it appeared to be the otherwise untouched room of a typical college boy: messy with clothes lying about and the bed unmade. Even the letter he had written and left behind still lay on the bathroom counter with the pen next to it.

I took a deep breath and walked straight to Patrick's closet. Resolved to find the answers I so desperately craved, I started at one end and touched each piece of his clothing, sifting through every pocket. Nothing. Next, I went to his desk and emptied all the drawers and flipped through all of his notebooks. Nothing out of the norm there either. I dumped his trashcan upside down and rummaged through everything in it. The only arresting item was an empty pack of cigarettes. Normally, that would have triggered an intense conversation between us. But in that moment, I instead felt endeared to him. He had chosen to experiment with something that, to my knowledge, his brothers never had, and though I didn't like it in the least, I wanted to tell him I understood and wasn't disappointed or mad. It didn't make sense, but that's what I felt.

After examining every last object in his room and finding nothing to indicate that he had been depressed or otherwise unstable, I sat on the floor and picked up his coat that still lay in a pile where he left it. Like a baby reaching for the comfort of her blanket, I brought it to my face and inhaled his scent. Suddenly, from the depths of my soul, a cry unlike any other that had ever emanated from me rose up and filled Patrick's room. It wasn't like the hysteria that overtook me when I found out he was dead. It was from a different place—as if releasing a part of myself that had newly died, the pain and the heartbreak and the veritable nightmare of a mother facing the truth that her child was gone.

❧

SOMETIME AFTER WE returned home from Indiana, Matthew came into my room.

"I know you'll want this," he said tenderly.

In his hand was Patrick's journal. I had forgotten that Danielle had encouraged him to start one, and I hadn't remembered seeing it in his room. But Matthew had found it, and, concerned it might be too soon that day for me to be faced with it, made sure it was packed with his things.

After Matthew left the room, I climbed into bed and held the journal for a few minutes. I was still in a place of longing for answers, and I was so grateful to have this piece of Patrick to connect to. I ran my hand over the cover and brought it to my face. Then I gingerly opened it to the first page. It felt strange to read Patrick's words, as if I was invading his privacy, but his handwriting brought him back to life and I suddenly felt his spirit with me. *Read it, Mom*, he seemed to whisper. *It will help you understand. I know how much you need that now.*

I read the first few entries, each of which reflected how

much he missed his dad and grampa, but it was this one that confirmed what I wholeheartedly believed, and what his best friend Cody confided to me as well: that Patrick never had any intention of taking his own life.

November 30, 2008

Home is so different without Dad. My Mom picked me up and we met Matt & Anne. My Mom brought one of Dad's dress shirts for me to wear . . . I love wearing my Dad's clothes, it feels like he's with me in a way.

When I got home it was obvious my Mom put almost all pictures of my Dad away. She says she's just not ready to look at them every day. I can understand that in a way but was so sad to see them missing. All of us cope with this pretty differently. When I'm home, it's the only place I want to be. Just being around family is so comforting to me.

We had Thanksgiving at Aunt Patti's and I thought about Dad the majority of the night. I stepped out to look at the sunset and talked to my Dad and just missed him so much. They all made it so special.

A few weeks after my Dad passed away we received a bag of his belongings. My Mom and I opened the bag together. My heart broke seeing his shirt and shoes and all his belongings. Dad didn't have a distinct smell but I breathed his shirt scent in and could just feel him in it.

My mom held and stared at the wedding ring she gave him. My heart just ached. There were two notes: " I cannot face the future. I am sorry." and " Leave all my possessions to my wife Mary T. Odgers. Signed Bruce K. Odgers." I hated that he didn't write anything sincere or . . . I just can't explain. He must have felt so bad and was not thinking in his right mind. I know the depression took over. My Dad would never do this. It hurts so bad to think how bad my Dad felt. There was a Patron label in the bag, which makes me think he needed the alcohol to sort of make his decisions. This all just makes no sense for my Dad, not at all.

The police report said there was a brown handled knife too. I cringed at those words. I cried and asked my mom if he used it to cut his wrists. She said yes. All I did was picture my Dad in that hotel room and a graphic scene.

A few days later Mom said there was more to the cause of death. She asked if I was ready to know and I said no. A few days after that Matt, Anne, and I were walking on the beach and Matt brought up that I shouldn't want to know. He said he knew and it was just too much. I agreed that I didn't want to know.

I spent two weeks at Purdue then went to Oklahoma for another memorial for Dad. My Dad's parents didn't even really bring it up. They were comforting but it was just strange they didn't talk about it.

We stayed at Uncle John's. I feel so much closer to him. He's doing what Dad would do if the circumstances were flipped . . .

When I went home this past week for Thanksgiving, I was home by myself for a brief period of time. I had been thinking every day of how my Dad really did take his life. I searched the entire house for a death certificate and finally came upon it.

I was mad at myself for finding out but also glad that I couldn't wonder any longer. It ached to see the words "cause of death: suicide." The cause of death was "hanged self with belt."

I can barely even write these words but doing it will really help in these months to come. I've read it's normal for one to not even want to say the word "suicide." My heart just ached and once again all I could do was envision my Dad with a belt around his neck. Why? Why? Why?

It is normal, but I have been a little angry at Dad. Why would he leave my Mom with so many things? Why did he have to leave all of us? Dad was so depressed and in so much pain. His last days must have been the toughest of his life. Something in his brain got triggered and made him not Dad anymore. He loved me so much in our last conversation. I wish I knew how bad it was. I would have told him how much I loved him.

I need to find the time to tell my mom I know of the circumstances. I told Matt I know. It helps talking to Matt about Dad.

I think about you all the time, Dad. I _will_ get these next 3 weeks completed. I _will_ make you proud, Dad. I miss you so much. I am so proud that you were and always will be my Dad. Please be here to listen and still try to guide me the right way in life.

Right now everything's nothing without you but one day we will learn to be on this earth without you. I can't wait to be with you in heaven. I know you're finally at peace with no worries at all. We will all take care of Mom. We love you so much, Dad.

Yes, Patrick did say he couldn't wait to be with his dad in heaven.

But I knew in my heart, after everything else he'd expressed in that entry, that he meant it for the far distant future.

IN THE WEEKS that followed, some days were so rough that I could hardly see clear of the pain. Other days, I felt uplifted by someone or something and felt a ray of hope. Every day, I found a reason to trust in God—to remember he was with me, and that he was with Bruce and my sweet Patrick. I was also comforted by the fact that Bruce, Dad, and Patrick all had each other, as much as it hurt that they were no longer here with me.

I also began to see that while I *did* matter to Bruce and Patrick—and even to Matthew and David—how they felt about me or my opinions paled in comparison to their personal needs and desires. My ego had me believing that I'd been paramount in the decisions they made, but that was a lie. I had put this unspeakable burden on myself, only to realize that I didn't have the amount of power I thought I did. It hurt to believe I was more insignificant in the lives of those I loved than I had always believed. But at the same time, it lifted a tremendous weight from me to realize that their decisions weren't my fault—that Bruce and Patrick, in particular, made them from pain inside themselves that I had no control over.

MEMORIES OF PATRICK blessed my days in waves, as if his life was playing out for me, scene by scene, from the time he was a little boy. Although it broke my heart that we would never make any more earthly memories together, it filled my heart with joy to relive these precious moments of our lives together.

I remembered how, on the day he was born, he turned toward the sound of my voice while in his father's arms. It was instant love, instant bonding, between mother and son.

At age two, instead of saying "Up," he would raise his spindly little arms toward me and say, "I hold you, Mommy." And hold me he did. If I had unwrapped my arms, not that I ever did, I knew he wouldn't fall because he would be melded to me as if he was part of me.

At age three, I remember how he became enamored with a friend he called Chris Labow (at least I think that was how his name was spelled). He made it clear that they were good friends, and I naturally assumed he was a little boy from school. Soon, however, I discovered that "Chris" joined us at the dinner table or sat next to Patrick in the car. One would think that with two brothers, Patrick didn't need an imaginary friend, but Chris became a more and more present companion. I'd ask Patrick questions about him, and although Chris was often "there" during my inquiries, he wasn't very forthcoming with details. What I remember most is that Patrick would be very serious about Chris's presence while the rest of us were entertained.

Chris was my fourth son until Patrick was about five or six, when suddenly, Patrick stopped referring to him.

"Is Chris here?" I asked one day at the table.

"No," Patrick said very matter of factly. "Chris died."

"He did?" I said, seeming alarmed. "How?"

Patrick shrugged. "On a roller-coaster."

He had a solemn look on his face, but that was always how he looked when he talked about Chris. I scanned his sweet features for traces of emotion, but there were none.

"I'm so sorry, honey," I offered.

But Patrick just stared ahead. "I don't want to talk about it," he said, making it clear the conversation was closed.

In the subsequent days, I had watched him carefully, not worried but checking for signs of grief or anything related.

There was nothing.

That was simply the end of Chris.

Whatever had prompted him to make up a friend, hold on to him for nearly three years, and then display such a nebulous response upon his demise baffled me.

It wasn't the last time Patrick would leave me with more questions than answers.

IN MY PERSISTENT quest for peace, I did things you might imagine a grieving mother would do—pray, journal, read books—but I was so desperate to find some connection with Patrick that I also opened my mind to things I'd never considered before, one of which was seeking guidance from intuitives. The truth was, it didn't matter if what they said was true; I just wanted to feel better. I had been hoping that Patrick would somehow come to me, but he hadn't yet and I couldn't understand why he would stay away from me when I longed for him so intensely. So, I consulted a few different intuitives to help me gain some level of solace, each of whom encouraged me to continue being patient.

The morning after Patrick died, David had come into my room crying and said that Patrick had visited him in a dream. "He told me he was okay, Mom," he said, as if giving me news that would miraculously make my sadness go away.

I was curious as to why Patrick had visited David, not

Matthew, when the two of them were so close. But then I realized precisely why: Matthew was always very tender and protective of me, and he might not have told me about the dream for fear that it would upset me. David, on the other hand, didn't possess those same filters. Patrick had chosen David, I reasoned, because he was sure to relay the message to me. Why he didn't just come directly to me, I didn't understand. But then it started to become clear.

Sometime after David's encounter, Patrick began coming to me in dreams at the age of his death. He wouldn't look at me, but I kept trying to get to him, desperate to tell him not to carry out his plan. After the third dream or so, he suddenly appeared as a three-year-old, with his straight blond hair and perfect little baby teeth when he smiled. He made direct eye contact with me, and he answered every question truthfully that I asked, even if it wasn't what I wanted to hear.

I didn't understand at the time why the earlier dreams had been so different from this one, so I returned to one of the intuitives and shared my experience with her. During this particular visit, she was able to channel Patrick.

She closed her eyes and was silent for a moment as she tapped into Patrick's energy. "He says that your grief is like a magnet attracting him to you, depleting his celestial energy."

My heart sank. "What does that mean?"

"It's not good that you're pulling on him," she continued. "He says he won't come to you in dreams anymore until you accept that he's gone."

Accept that he's gone? I couldn't believe Patrick would ask that of me. Although I got it on an intellectual level, it felt unimaginable.

"I know it's hard," the intuitive said. "But he's being very clear. He wants you to know that he's okay . . . but he can't move on unless you stop trying to pull his soul toward you."

Anguished over the idea of releasing Patrick from me, the little boy who always clung to me so tightly, I wished I could drift into a deep sleep and awaken in five years, with the void no longer present in the same torturous way. But I also knew this process of grieving was necessary, as much as I doubted I could ever move through it.

Weeks before in the viewing room, on the day of his twenty-first birthday, I had told Patrick that I accepted his choice, but it was at the suggestion of Florence. I didn't mean it then and I didn't know how I could mean it now. Yet, hearing the request relayed from Patrick, I felt determined to try.

I left the intuitive's home seeing my world through fresh eyes, feeling a new direction had been handed to me. I felt wholly unequipped to honor Patrick's wish, but there was a renewed energy in me that day. He had said he might come to me again if I was able to let go, and the idea of that reward was enough to motivate me.

What was so unthinkable was finding a place for the pain, of being tormented by not being able to hold my son physically, to see his face or hear his voice or catch a trace of his scent. Longings that, according to Patrick, were disrupting his energy field, whatever that meant. Because of that, and because the five senses no longer applied when it came to how I experienced Patrick, I was forced to learn to connect to him in a spiritual sense. It could never compare to physically holding him, but I was obsessed with finding a way to survive being without him.

Slowly, deliberately, I chose to think of Patrick's presence as a spiritual being, one I could talk to openly and imagine was with me at times, sharing my emotions but not in the same agonizing way I had before. Instead of begging God for peace, I learned to try and feel Patrick's presence, pretending we were hanging out together in a new way. I could share how I was feeling, tell him things he might find amusing, express that I was really trying but that I still found it difficult. In this way, I could find some sense of balance. I won't pretend it was easy, and some people may have found my methods to be a bit eccentric, but I did what I needed to do to cope, and sometimes that meant imagining Patrick was still here.

For example, when I returned to work at the hospital, a patient might ask me personal questions during a brief check, such as if I had any children. Knowing the conversation would go no further, I would simply say, "Yes, I have three sons."

Other times, when I would meet someone new and they would ask if I had kids, I would say I had one son with special needs who was doing great and had a steady job, another who was in law school, and another who was "finding his way." It wasn't exactly a lie—Patrick was, in his new state of being, finding his way. But it allowed me to escape trying to pretend I only had two sons, which felt completely wrong to say, or to try to explain that my third child had died, without having to go into the details of how. Still other times I could couch the topic by saying, "I have three sons—Patrick passed when he was twenty-one—" and then continue to describe David and Matthew. Sometimes the person would want to circle back to Patrick and express their condolences; others got the message that it was easiest not to go there. When the person was bold enough to ask how Patrick died, I had to decide in the moment what I felt comfortable saying. It was much too complicated to say that he took his life accidentally; trying to explain that sounded like a pitiable theory concocted by a disbelieving mother who couldn't accept the truth. Even though I knew Patrick never meant to die, it was futile to try to get someone I'd just met, or even someone I'd known for a while, to believe

that. Even if I'd known they'd be sympathetic and give cre-
dence to my story, it was just too much for me. Plus, some
people were simply too inquisitive to read the social cues that
their questions weren't welcome. So I did—or didn't—bring up
Patrick on any given day, depending on what I could handle in
the moment. This allowed me to navigate the new version of
my life the best I could in the public arena.

But our now family of three was a different story.

After Patrick died, I was riddled with worry about how
David and Matthew would cope with losing their father and
brother so close together. I prayed they wouldn't fall prey to
dark thoughts and follow Bruce and Patrick's lead, that God
would instill in them a will to survive. They were my entire
world and my reason for living. Although nearly impossible to
see some days, I believed our diminished family had immense
vitality and potential, and I didn't want my boys to lose those
qualities in their grief.

Besides the fears that plagued me, it was almost as if I had to
"start over" with David and Matthew. And I wasn't the only one
who felt out of balance with only two sons; they felt out of balance too. That wobbly bike they had been before Patrick came
along and made it a steady tricycle had once again been replaced
by that precarious two-wheeler; the absence of Patrick changed
their dynamic all over again. The lighthearted buffer that Patrick
provided, the prankster and free-spirited brother David and
Matthew both found endearing, was gone. Their "something in
common" reverted back to "little in common," making Patrick's
absence an even more glaring hole than it already was.

One day, when both David and Matthew were home, I
attempted to bring them together by asking them about
Patrick. I had still been struggling to try to understand the psyche of my youngest son, and I wondered if perhaps there was

something I'd been unaware of as his mother that his brothers had known all along.

"Did you guys see Patrick as the impulsive type?" I asked.

From the looks on their faces, you would have thought I asked them if their brother was really a boy.

"Are you kidding?" they said in unison. In an instant, they were on the same page, proceeding to offer multiple examples that horrified me as I realized *how* impulsively my son had conducted his life at times.

"Stop," I implored. "I *don't* want to know this stuff." I was happy to see the momentary connection between David and Matthew, but as a mother, visualizing Patrick getting drunk and doing things that were totally out of character, or knowing about crazy risks he took, unsettled me. I walked away feeling like I wanted to protect myself from knowing too much and collapsed onto a chair in the patio.

I desperately wanted to erase what the boys had just told me, but as those examples—along with the frequently perplexing times I shared with Patrick—flashed in my mind one after the other, that cloudy lens through which I often viewed my youngest suddenly became crystal clear: what I perceived as confusion on his part for the way he made some of his decisions couldn't have been more wrong. I finally saw Patrick for what he really was: a purely black-and-white thinker who could easily place his actions into completely unrelated boxes. I could never understand how a person could be so committed to something that served himself only, but Patrick was simply decisive, come what may. That night in his bedroom at Purdue, he decided to experience what his father must have experienced in his last minutes of life, and though he didn't mean to go as far as Bruce did, no rationale would have stopped him from carrying out the experiment. He needed answers. He got an idea of how to get those answers, at least to some degree. Then, as Patrick always did, he leapt forward without ever looking back.

For me, it was that first day of preschool all over again, when I as the mother was left longing for comfort from my child as I watched him go so boldly into the world, with no second thoughts, no fear of the unknown, leaving me behind in a way I'd never anticipated.

Only this time, it was permanent.

All those years ago, and on certain occasions since, my headstrong, decisive boy had left me with a slightly wounded heart, one that felt pierced in the moment but would recover with time.

Now, it seemed impossible to imagine that my heart would ever recover.

Impossible because it wasn't left with merely a bruise or an abrasion that would heal in time. It had been shattered, with impact like no other, into a million pieces.

I didn't know it would be the last time
that I'd hold you so close,
tell you I loved you;
that I was so proud of you.
We were hurting badly, yet
courageously, you took the first step.
You were the shining moment
that beckoned to tomorrow
maybe the chance of happiness again.
Brave enough to go back to Purdue
and step into our new life,
you hugged me so close
there on the curb at Lindbergh

with your suitcase
and the pink paper envelope in your fist
to read after you got on the plane.
That would tell you once again
how much I loved you,
how proud of you I was,
how you could call me when you landed.
I would come to you
or you could call me tomorrow.
I'd make a reservation for you to come home
to our broken home,
the home that needed healing,
the home that with you in my arms that minute
just might feel a breath of life again.
"Don't read it til you're on the plane," I said
with my face against yours.
I whispered those words to you
then I let go
for the last time
that I would ever touch you.
Oh God, if I'd only known,
I would have kept driving
and driving and driving, past the airport
just to have you next to me
for a little longer.
Because you did go back.
You did settle in.
You got an internship and
we planned a trip that spring,
you and I.
You promised to be my new business partner,
until your sadness, laced with alcohol,

let you relax into your grief,
the grief that weighed your soul down.
And you said goodbye.
I know you didn't mean it,
but that's what happens after a party
when your heart is in such pain
for your Dad.
If only I could go back to that minute
that I didn't know was the last.

michael

$\mathcal{B}$ARELY TWO YEARS LATER, IN 2011, STILL REELING from the losses of Bruce and Patrick, I was hit with yet another unexpected blow: the loss of my brother, Michael. It had not always been an easy road with him, but he and I had shared a special bond, and my memories of him reached all the way back to the day I was introduced to him . . .

I PEERED DOWN the long, shiny hallway in anticipation. Over the past several days, I'd heard grownups in hushed voices speak of blood loss and the baby being born feet first, scaring me and making me wonder how my mother would look when I saw her next. At four years old, I thought little about the baby; I had missed my mother terribly while she was in the hospital and couldn't wait to rush into her arms. But when my parents materialized at the end of the corridor, my grandma gave my hand a gentle squeeze, then looked sternly down at my sisters and me and told us quietly to wait.

I couldn't take my eyes off my mother. She was wearing a familiar green shirt dress—one with a belt that accentuated her waistline. I hadn't seen her stomach without a baby in it for a long time, and the belt made her look small. She was holding my new baby brother like a beloved treasure, and my dad—who was always big and strong in my eyes—carried a gentle-

ness about him that couldn't be missed, one I didn't recall seeing before. I liked the feeling it gave me, that sense of kindness
he seemed to emanate. But it was my mother catching sight of
Joyce, Patti, and me and her face lighting up that flooded me
with happiness. After she'd endured a difficult delivery of an
infant who was four weeks overdue and a seven-day stay in the
maternity ward, I was finally getting my mother back. I was
also getting a brother for the first time, and I was admittedly
curious what our new little novelty would be like.

Michael Jude was a gentle and good-natured baby, so
when our next brother came along only thirteen months later,
I expected him—in my five-year-old naiveté—to be like
Michael. But as they grew, David, though he looked in many
ways like Michael, was husky in comparison to Michael's
slimness and showed a striking contrast in personality. While
Michael was a sweet, endearing, and quiet boy who was always up for being good company to his sisters, David was
more of a tornado, a rough-and-tumble kid who was noisy
and short on attention. Though we each bonded with our
siblings in our own ways, I came to realize as a young girl
that I could never hope to keep up with the highly masculine
"all boy" David, so I found my solace in Michael's more gentle
company—which made for a perfect partnership in my inspired performances.

By the time he was four or five, Michael, with his interested and cooperative manner, willingly became the backup
singer for my song and dance routines.

"Okay, Michael," I might say, "when I give you the sign, I
want you to jump off the chair and sing 'Baby you and me,'
and then just dance 'til I tell you to stop."

With a point of my finger at the proper time, Michael
would let loose with the practiced one liner and shake his

little booty as instructed, adding to my illusions that I was a bona fide singer worthy of a pack of screaming fans. His endless patience for getting it right and his enthusiasm for being a part of it all made us an unstoppable duo in my mind.

Patti, on the other hand, had a completely different view of Michael as a sidekick.

One day, the two of them had stolen away to the bathroom and closed the door—a sure sign of imminent trouble—with Patti claiming they were plotting some sort of adventure. Suddenly, the house was full of Michael's screams.

"I don't know how it happened," Patti said in hysterics. "I just turned around and there he was—falling out the window!"

Michael had landed on the air conditioning unit, and his bleeding face was alarming. My mother quickly and carefully laid him down on the kitchen table (which in retrospect is funny that my mom, a former nurse, often used our kitchen table as a gurney to assess not only our family's injuries, but the neighborhood kids' scrapes and bruises as well). Stitches were in order, creating a full afternoon of excitement for us kids.

It wasn't until later that the true story came out.

Michael and Patti were constructing a fort, and in order to be a member, one had to fulfill the requirements—the first of which was jumping out the bathroom window. Patti, being the one in charge, suggested Michael go first. Eager to gain entry into the elite club, he climbed onto the window sill and, legs dangling, peered downward. Fearful, he hesitated. But Patti wasn't giving him an out. She gave him a nudge . . . and the rest was history.

At the time, the bloody event was traumatizing, but years later, we all laughed as Michael told and retold the story of his boot camp experience to "gain entry into the fort." Looking back, I don't know how he survived all the bossing and antics from his three older sisters who harbored—and executed—endless plans for him.

WITH FIVE LITTLE ones under the age of seven, the pressures of parenting and of my dad's career mounted. But every so often, Dad would take us out individually for special time with him—an idea my mom hatched. Dad agreed with her that between his busy schedule and having little spare time, he was missing out on building a relationship with each of his kids. So, she set up our "dates" as time permitted, and we each got to look forward to these treasured one-on-one outings with our dad. Everyone, that is, except for Michael.

Because David and Michael were only thirteen months apart, their scheduled outings were always a package deal, but Michael didn't seem to mind that his brother was part of his "Dad time." I think my dad was grateful, too, that they never had to be alone.

Once, after returning from their afternoon out, I heard Dad, who was clearly disgruntled, say to Mom, "They didn't eat what we ordered. And Michael . . . well . . . that kid is just different."

"Oh, Dave," my mother said with a flip of her hand, disappearing into the kitchen.

My dad continued shaking his head, mumbling, "All Michael kept saying over and over was, 'Today is *my* special day out.'"

I remember observing his body language and apparent agitation, confused about why that was such a big deal; it *was* supposed to be Michael's special day out. Why it irritated my dad so much that Michael kept repeating it was lost on me.

I didn't realize at the time that it was more than that that got under my dad's skin, something much deeper that wouldn't be apparent—and that I wouldn't understand—until Michael was a young man.

AFTER CAROL WAS born in March of 1966, we moved to our new station in Washington DC. For my father's career, it was stupendous. But for six kids under the age of sixteen, it was confining with very little freedom to just be kids.

Our home was assigned stewards to cook and clean, and the compound was guarded by Marine security guards, keeping us from wandering beyond the gates into the slums that dotted southeast Washington DC in the early 1970s. On occasion one of our stewards—who was only eighteen himself—would walk the boys up to Capitol Hill or to one of the Smithsonian museums. In between, my brothers had time on their hands to get into mischief on the compound.

There were five sets of military quarters in addition to the majestic historic Commandant's House at the end of the expansive parade deck. One of the quarters was used as lodging for bachelor officers and other official guests visiting the compound—and it was outfitted with a well-stocked bar. We didn't know it at the time, but Michael and David regularly visited that bar one summer, only with very different results.

Both boys had gotten a kick out of getting away with sneaking alcohol. But while David would drink a little out of the bottles and laugh with Michael at the effects it had on them, he would typically lose interest in favor of watching TV or taking a nap. Michael, on the other hand, found his happy place in those bottles. The awful-tasting mixtures they concocted took a hold of him, giving him an uncommon sense of peace and serenity. Though he wasn't more than ten, an age when he should have been carefree with no worries, that fleeting feeling of bliss became a necessity, and he began doing whatever he could to sneak nips—or more—of liquor. It wasn't long before he developed an edge that overshadowed his previously sweet disposition, frequently saying and doing things that offended my siblings—and even me—at times. He talked back in a way that was unacceptable to my parents and caused rage in my father, and the repercussions were often grave, igniting physical brutality between my dad and Michael that I found impossible to shake. An unsettling pattern became established between the two of them, and while my mother preferred to pretend nothing was wrong, it was clear that something was going terribly awry.

A few years later, after we'd moved to Colorado Springs where we now had ten acres of wide open space that included a pond, horses, and a lush, thriving garden of rhubarb, tomatoes, and a plethora of other gifts from the earth, Michael got into a serious accident on his shiny new mini-bike. He spent six weeks in the ICU in traction, with both legs broken badly and his right arm suspended high above his head, as if perpetually waiting to be called on by a teacher. Dad was in Okinawa, Japan, at the time, and once we were certain Michael was going to survive, Mom told him there was no need to come home.

When Michael was released from the hospital in time for Christmas, we were all overjoyed that he was able to leave his wheelchair and sit on the living room floor with us amongst the Christmas chaos. Dad had sent several gifts from overseas, and Michael lavished in the attention, especially from our dad. All the hostility between them seemed to evaporate through the love that was sent from across the world in the form of gifts and phone calls of encouragement, and the apparent father-son bond that blossomed gave me hope for them that I thought was lost forever—one I believed the rest of my family felt too.

It was a few months before Michael could walk and go back to school, so various friends and neighbors hung out at his bedside entertaining him with local gossip and random gifts. Two of those neighbors were boys a few years older than Michael—and the "gifts" they brought came in the form of illegal drugs. None of us knew it at the time, but at the tender age of thirteen, my little brother was finding escape in the euphoria of mind-altering substances.

AFTER SEVERAL MONTHS in Japan, my dad returned and we moved to San Diego for his next duty assignment. Michael made some new friends and appeared to settle down a bit, and my dad—reaching the apex of professional dedication and years of hard work—was promoted to brigadier general. Not long after, he received orders to the First Marine Brigade in Kaneohe, Hawaii.

My sister Joyce and I stayed behind in California, struggling through a tearful goodbye to my parents and four younger siblings—but perhaps worst for me was seeing Michael amble down the jetway toward the plane, last in the line of six. Tall and slim, with long, stylish hair that reflected the hippie-influenced mid-seventies, he was a handsome young man despite the slight limp and scarred right arm that hung crooked as he carried his travel bag. He was as healed physically as anyone expected him to be, and I remember thinking that moving on to this next adventure held so much promise for him.

It was a blessing I didn't know that our family, with Michael the impetus of the downward spiral, would unravel to a tenuous thread yet again.

❧

MY PARENTS' NEW home in paradise was a beautiful set of quarters right on the Pacific Ocean, with a huge grassy yard that separated them from the rocky cliffs. Both Mom and Dad were completely immersed in the duties, both socially and professionally, of a brigadier general, and the kids were all enrolled in their respective schools. But it wasn't long before Michael found his way once again into the wrong crowd. He began using and selling drugs, something that was a potential career-breaker for my dad. By the time my parents caught wind of it, Michael had already slipped in school and lost his footing in reality. There was simply no reaching him. Numerous altercations ensued between him and my dad, the worst landing my father in the emergency room after hitting his head and requiring stitches.

Being three thousand miles away and immersed in my own world of relative adolescent freedom, I ached for my little brother—and the tension I knew his actions brought down on my family—but was unequipped to do much of anything for him. The closeness we had always shared was severed in a certain way by our geographical distance, so it was with both trepidation and hope that I arrived in Hawaii in December of 1975 for my sister Joyce's wedding.

Although Michael was still my sweet and sensitive brother, he was detached and distant. He had caused a lot of upheaval for my siblings, and the animosity they felt for him weighed on our reunion. We interacted with each other, but I was naïve at the time about the effects of drugs, so I chalked up the shift in his behavior to more of a teenage phase than a deeper, ongoing problem.

Joyce got married in a lovely island-inspired ceremony,

followed by a reception on the Pacific Ocean. Our cousins, the Thomases, had flown in from San Diego and were treated to a rented military beach house just walking distance from my parents' home.

A few days before the wedding, my Aunt Jane appeared raving on our doorstep.

"We came back after a short walk on the beach and the glass window on the front door was shattered!"

My father quickly ushered her inside as we all bounded down the stairs and gathered around. "Is anybody hurt?" he asked.

"No," she cried. "But we have every reason to believe it was Michael who did it!"

Though nothing was stolen, the window of their cottage had been the entry point for an intruder, and all eyes turned to Michael. Despite the bloody scratches on his arms, he vehemently denied his involvement, offering a dozen excuses why it wasn't him. It was clear that no one believed him, but Michael continued to deny it. No final verdict was ever reached, and although the disquiet gradually faded into a glorious wedding, the near-collective bitterness toward Michael remained vivid. While I wanted to believe him, it was achingly clear that he had collapsed the bridge for the last time between himself and some of our distant family.

AT THE END of our duty station in Hawaii, in the summer of 1978, Dad received new orders to be the inspector general of the Marine Corps in Washington DC. After my parents found a home in Vienna, Virginia, Dad's travels of the world's Marine Corps facilities began—and my mother was left with four children to tend to largely on her own, one of whom was Michael, who had once again become totally out of control.

The following February, the family returned to San Diego for another blessed occasion: my wedding to Bruce. But instead of being greeted by smiles and outstretched arms and expressions of delight at the airport, I was immediately thrust into a screaming match between Dad and the boys. My excitement to see them and to share my wedding celebration was instantly overshadowed by feelings of dread I hoped had been left behind. I couldn't understand what my brothers had done wrong. All I saw was my dad stretched as emotionally tight as I'd ever seen him.

Months prior, when Bruce called my dad to ask his permission to marry me—and received it—I excitedly grabbed the phone afterward. But before I could say a word, my dad commanded the conversation.

"You'll plan your wedding and have anything you want," he said, "but you have to do it alone."

"But, Dad," I argued, "I need Mom here to help me, even if it's just for a few days to get things planned out."

Dad was firm. "Mom's needed here with the kids."

My disappointment was palpable. Feeling both hurt and embarrassed that I didn't have the maternal support other girls had for their special day, I momentarily hoisted blame on Michael, but then quickly shifted my resentment onto my parents. *Why wasn't the problem with Michael getting solved?* I wondered. *Why does my wedding have to be the casualty of their dysfunction?*

IN THE NEXT months, I muddled through my wedding plans. My dad made two trips out to see me, hitching a ride in the backseat of an F-4 fighter jet. On one trip, he arranged for me to meet with a priest to officiate the wedding; on the other, he took me out to buy my wedding dress. Not the kind of man to enjoy dress shopping—let alone wedding dress shopping—when I tried on the first one, he said, "It's great! Let's get it."

Intent on making a thoughtful decision about such a big purchase, I said, "No, let's look at more."

He acquiesced, but by the end of the afternoon, we returned to that initial store and bought the first dress I'd tried on, laughing that he'd been right to love it after all.

THE FOLLOWING JUNE, newlyweds Bruce and I took our first trip together to Virginia to see my family. Dad was in Europe fulfilling his duties as the inspector general, and Mom was wearing her usual cloak of denial.

One of the family cars parked out front was dented in multiple places and full of empty beer cans.

"Where's your new car?" I asked my mom.

She cast her eyes downward with a sigh. "Michael wrecked it. He's just so reckless."

My forehead creased. "What does Dad say about it?"

"He says he can't be around him and the IG travel is a blessing."

I looked my mother directly in the eyes. "Mom. Someone has to do something. Michael's out of control. The other car looks like a drunkard's been driving it. There's a good chance Michael won't be graduating with his class next week. Haven't you noticed?"

She paused, then responded in a flat, distant voice. "No, he's just doing what boys do. And it's the clumsiness from his accident that causes him to be the worst driver. It'll all be fine. I'm sure it's nothing."

I wanted to scream and shake her. But when I looked deeper into her eyes, I saw the helplessness there and wanted to hug her so tightly that all her fears would go away.

If only it could have been that easy.

DESPITE FORESHADOWING TO the contrary, Michael did receive his high school diploma, followed by a bachelor's degree from the University of Texas at Arlington, and later a master's degree in human resources. My family had moved by this time to Plano, Texas, near where Bruce and I were living after he started his career with Delta.

At first, Michael connected with us reluctantly and showed obvious signs of a rough lifestyle. He had a bloated, ruddy look about him that exceeded the "freshman fifteen" students often gained in college, looking more to me like the "toxic twenty." Seeing his hands tremble ferociously, I feared he was lost yet again and had slipped into the darkness of addiction.

Over time, however, Michael began a routine of driving to our house every Sunday, one he became as faithful to as he had to various drugs throughout his life. Only he didn't arrive high or strung out; he had no telltale marks on his arms, nor did he exhibit the behaviors of an addict. In fact, he couldn't have been kinder or more attentive during those eagerly anticipated weekend visits.

Early in our Sunday afternoon chats, he admitted to me that my parents were only in touch with him on rare occasions.

"Mom took me to college," he said with a sad laugh,

"checked me into the dorm, bought me a meal ticket, and I never heard from her again."

I immediately had the sense that with us, Michael had found some sort of sanctuary. He loved our growing family and relished being there for me when Bruce was gone for long trips. A constant source of encouragement, he always lent a caring ear to my worries about child rearing, and we found laughter in retelling old stories and recalling the good times, however minimal they were.

But there was something else. I had suspected for a while but felt more certain during our talks that Michael was hiding who he really was: a gay man who had not only been held hostage by growing up with a stern military father and the edicts of the Catholic Church around marriage and family, but who had come of age during a time when being gay was mostly frowned upon in society, even abhorred. What's more, Texas couldn't have been a worse place for him; he was often beaten up by cowboys who cruised the gay bar scene, looking to make their views on homosexuality known.

My father had repeatedly remarked that Michael was "different"; he couldn't articulate it, but his eldest son, in manner and personality, had planted unease in him. For Michael, attempting to embrace his true identity would have surely been rejected in a traditional military and religious family such as ours. I didn't ask him about it directly, though, and he didn't volunteer any information to confirm it. It was simply a feeling I had, one the more I pondered, the more I realized his stifled—and possibly undesired—identity was an understandable source of the self-destructive path he'd unwittingly chosen for most of his life.

※

DURING MY SECOND pregnancy, Michael hit rock bottom. I didn't know exactly what the circumstances were, but Bruce retrieved him and brought him to our house. Through a fog of inebriation, he cried about how disappointed he was with himself, yet adamantly denied any alcohol or drug use—the same way he had denied having anything to do with the break-in at the cottage the day of Joyce's wedding.

"Hey, Michael," I had said nonchalantly, months after the incident when I thought the emotions had died down enough for the truth. "What was the story with the break-in at the Thomases' beach house?"

"I have no idea," he maintained with a shrug.

Then later, "That beach house thing . . . I still don't get what happened," I had ventured.

Without missing a beat, he said, "It was bizarre how all the attention was on me right away."

I nodded, then squinted slightly. "But you had scratches that looked like they were from broken glass."

"Yeah, it was all so weird," he reasoned, non-defensively. "I'd gotten those scratches from the coral reef that morning. Like, I'm sure I wouldn't have broken into *their* house of all places. I was a scapegoat for some reason."

And now here he was again, still professing his innocence, even with the alcohol escaping in acrid plumes when he spoke. His unwillingness to be truthful was inconceivable to me, and being concerned about his presence in a home with a toddler, we put him on a plane that night to my parents' house in Virginia. Security confiscated a bottle of vodka from his bag, and he arrived—to my parents' dismay and humiliation—hungover. They immediately checked him into a rehab facility, where they prayed for short-term detoxification, but held little hope for any long-term recovery.

The day after he was released from his stint in rehab, Michael was already looking for solace at the bottom of a bottle. It would be several more years before he dutifully entered AA and began to work diligently and with unparalleled dedication through the twelve steps.

Some months into his recovery process, he met a man named Luc. Luc was French and a former college professor at the Sorbonne, and though he was close to my father's age, the two of them immediately forged a deep and lasting bond. While on the surface it looked like a friendship that mirrored a father-son connection, I knew it was more than that. Truthfully, I felt relieved that Michael was finally living what seemed to be an authentic life and supported him completely. My mother had unconditionally accepted him, and my siblings had too—on varying levels—but my dad was horrified and sought help with a friend and former military colleague with a PhD in psychology, who calmed my dad's fears of being responsible for Michael's sexual preference.

OVER THE NEXT several years, as our little family grew to four, then five, Michael resumed his Sunday visits and loved his nephews as if they were the sons he would never have. When we bought our land in California and moved within a year, Michael was the person who made my insides ache; I knew I was going to miss him terribly. Although he had been a source of strife for everyone in the family, for me he brought encouragement, praise, and a friend I grew to rely on for emotional support. Leaving him was like leaving a part of my heart behind—but I was comforted by the fact that he was no longer alone.

Around that time, after Michael and Luc had essentially been a couple for years—and Michael had bravely maintained his sobriety—Michael was sparked to pursue a PhD in his field. But life was not always pleasant for male couples in the US, and having no real ties to home, Luc suggested that they move to France—and Michael accepted.

Luc and Michael spent twenty-one years together in their French idyll. Their fourth-floor flat consisted of three tiny rooms, endearingly organized and minimalistic. The elevator that creaked its way to their place held only two people or one person with luggage, but upon my first visit, I could appreciate the quaintness of it all. Michael learned to speak French beautifully (or so I thought—Luc apparently didn't agree!), and he and Luc enjoyed a small circle of dear friends: an Italian married couple, some singles, and a few relatives of Luc's. Michael found his niche in this world and it seemed that, having received the long-desired poultice of acceptance and the fortification of love, he had finally left addiction behind him for good.

MICHAEL AND I spoke every Sunday for years. We talked about his and Luc's travels and of course about my boys. But mostly we talked about life in general, and our take on things —like our upbringing. We often found ourselves laughing at some of the particulars, wondering, *What were Mom and Dad thinking?* In one conversation we discovered we had both embraced a common practice to clear our minds before sleep, or during stressful times when we needed to center our- selves—before meditation was widely used by most Ameri- cans. Michael quipped, "You know, I think we invented med- itation." After dishing about some of the oddities of our childhood, his comment struck me as hilarious and we both cracked up. Laughter was huge with us—sometimes it covered pain, and sometimes it was an expression of silliness we found in the shared experiences that were our glue. But there was also an undeniable sense of pride I felt in him—and of the fact that after all the years of struggle he'd endured, he was as proud as I was of his educational accomplishments, as well as of the way he had slowly mastered more than one language through the years.

After two decades together, Luc's health began to fail—and Michael began to fall apart. I heard it in his voice during our long-distance phone conversations—in the way he repeated himself and drew out his words. He was losing the love of his life, and I knew it was more than Michael could bear. It was as if the hard-won balance he had treasured for so long was being taken from him, a balance he'd never developed the skills to sustain by himself.

During that time was when Bruce got a job flying a wealthy man's private plane. One of their destinations was Cannes, and I tagged along as the flight attendant, hopeful to see Michael during the three weeks we would be on layover there. But Michael uncharacteristically said no, so my plans to comfort him in person were never fulfilled.

SOMETIME AFTER LUC'S health began its demise, he passed away quietly with my brother by his side.

Michael returned to America, deflated and lost. He moved into a house near my parents' and, in a magical spin of the coin, started to rebuild a relationship with them. It was as if my dad had completed his hard-fought journey of acceptance and was now actually enjoying his first-born son. A newfound peace developed between the two of them, and Michael found a calling in tending to my dad as he had tended to Luc. My dad grew to enjoy his company, taking frequent trips out for coffee with Michael and even giving him items of his clothing that Michael had expressed liking.

But despite the rosy exterior of Michael's post-Luc existence, he was suffering terribly on the inside. To try to disguise the grief that weighed on him, and that he feared my parents wouldn't fully understand, he had begun taking some of Luc's leftover prescription drugs. He had also procured medication for persistent back pain he was suffering. On one particular day, he took either too much of one or some combination of the two—a decision that proved to be catastrophic.

Michael and my father had one of their trips into town planned, and Michael drove, as he always did. But the prescription drugs he had taken that morning to ease both his physical and emotional pain marred his judgment, and he wasn't able to react fast enough. In a flash, Michael caused a near-fatal collision.

While Michael essentially walked away unharmed, the fact that my father was left a quadriplegic, dependent on a ventilator for every breath, was something my sisters and brother couldn't forgive. They placed the blame for the accident squarely on Michael and turned their backs on him for good, seeing him as nothing but an addict who was out of control. Everyone has their breaking point, and this was theirs. At the time, I had no idea that Michael's addiction had spawned gross disrespect toward my siblings and, at times, their children. But once the stories started circulating, I realized why there were no more second chances for him in their eyes. Sadly, that rejection nearly killed him.

With all of the animosity my family felt for Michael, I

knew from our history with him in Texas that this was not the whole of my brother. Through all the turbulence, he and I had built a lasting bond. My siblings didn't know the side of him that I did, so I didn't blame them for being unable to see him in any other way. And, despite the daggers being hurled in his direction, we all somehow understood that none of us could hate Michael more than he now hated himself.

For a short time after the accident, Michael lived nearby in San Diego. After I lost Bruce, Dad, and Patrick in a span of less than two months, he had frequently come over to be with me. One day, I was entering our townhouse through the garage when Michael was coming out. In my stuporous fog, he hugged me, then began telling me something. I don't recall what he said, all I remember is that I wanted to be attentive to him but had little energy for it. As I listened and half-heartedly responded, I felt self-centered and terrible; it wasn't the norm for me to go through the motions, but I was just too spent to be a good listener.

It was at that moment that Michael gently took my hand.

"Mary," he said, "I admire your strength so much. I just don't know how you're handling all this. You've given me an amazing example of the courage it takes to survive the unthinkable."

That was the Michael I loved.

Pure, unconditional, and so lovingly honest.

I lived on those words for years.

LITTLE MORE THAN two years later, on March 11, 2011, Pierre—a dear and wonderful man who would enable me to find love again—called to ask if he could come over. It was early in the morning, and he was oddly adamant about it, so I quickly showered, filled with curiosity. When he arrived, I invited him into the living room. He stood solemnly, shifting uncomfortably for a moment.

"Michael's gone," he said tenderly.

"Michael who?" I asked, as several Michaels I knew came into my head.

"Your brother," he said with a soft sigh. "Carol called me and said she didn't want you to be alone when you found out."

I immediately melted into uncontrollable sobs. Pierre was new in my life and hadn't met Michael, so he had no idea how to respond to my devastation. He sat beside me and put his arm around my shoulders, holding me close.

There had been a period in the last couple years when Michael had suddenly become unavailable for our long-held Sunday calls. I suspected that someone we both knew had said something untrue to poison him against me, and Michael eventually confessed to me that that's what had happened. Why he had absorbed this person's lie as truth I couldn't understand, but the love I had for him was still strong, and I found it easy to forgive him. It was Michael's sweet way to think the situation through and see it for what it truly was. He was deeply repentant, and I was relieved that it was finally all out in the open. But even though he apologized sincerely, and we affectionately reconciled, something had tainted our closeness, and we never quite found the loving rhythm we had cherished in the past.

"Did Carol say how he died?" I asked Pierre.

He paused thoughtfully. "It was a heart attack," he said, "in his sleep."

Whether it had been brought on by drugs or not, I didn't know. Later I found out that Michael had bought pizzas the night before for his friends, and his roommate remembered hearing him take a hot shower around two a.m., seeking relief from his searing back pain. It was possible he had accidentally taken too much pain medication and never woken up. But in that moment, all I knew was that my once sweet brother—the boy who sang and danced with me, who listened to my woes, who made me feel brave and resilient and amazing—was no longer on this earth with me.

Through my tears, I told Pierre about my brother—all the bad, all the good. I shared my frustrations about Michael, and also my deep, unconditional love for him.

Days later, I gave the eulogy at Michael's funeral. Afterward, we projected a pictorial montage of Michael that my nephew, Adam, helped me create. As the images flashed onto the screen, accompanied by the moving lyrics of "In My Life" by The Beatles, I sensed, glancing at the faces of my family, that they felt little but exhaustion; they seemed to be there merely for my mother's sake. I, however, felt every note of the music and resonated deeply with the touching chorus of the lyrics:

In my life, I'll love you more.

I realized then that I loved Michael more than enough to say goodbye, enough to accept that he had had enough of this world in his mere forty-nine years. And I've never had a truly sorrowful moment as a result of his passing, only happiness in knowing that in his divine form, he has the company of his beloved Luc, of Dad, of Patrick, of Bruce. And perhaps even more consoling—after a grueling entry into the world and an often tempestuous stay—is knowing that Michael is finally, fully, at peace.

m o m

❧

ROM THE OUTSIDE, A MARINE CORPS GENERAL falling for a fly-by-the-seat-of-her-pants, Mother Earth–type doesn't seem terribly likely. Yet that's exactly the girl my dad fell in love with: a spirited, active, headstrong woman who butted heads regularly with her mother, was the leader of two younger brothers, and embraced a rather Bohemian lifestyle that was the opposite of my father's idea of running a household and raising a family. Whether they were drawn together by their shared Catholic backgrounds, a common familiarity with military life, or a bit of magic that made their contrasting views appealing, in the nearly fifty years they were married, Helen Joyce Thomas and David Twomey couldn't have been more devoted to one another.

My father's military strictness and desire for order ruled our house when he was home. But when he wasn't, my mother seemed to fall contentedly into unstructured chaos: her rules were bendable, her punishments were learning opportunities, and her down-to-earth view of things was a magnet for anyone seeking solace in the walls of our home. Always willing to make room for one more at the table, she welcomed everyone, and she was never apologetic that our house often teemed with mayhem—lots of yelling, lots of laughter, and an always healthy dose of going with the flow was what a visitor could expect.

As the wife of a military man, going with the flow became my mother's modus operandi. If her presence was requested at an event, she was polished from head to toe, carrying out whatever role my father required. If people needed welcoming to a new duty station, she made it her business to see they were embraced. She obediently birthed and raised six children—frequently with the burden squarely on her while Dad traveled—and there was nothing my father asked of her that she would have refused to do. She packed our house and bundled up our family countless times when Dad was reassigned, never complaining. Almost staggeringly so, my mother was game for anything that would support her husband and his growing rank, and it was easy to see that she was his biggest—and most prized—asset.

What was not so easy to see was the pain she carried that shaped her into the exceedingly dutiful wife and overly optimistic woman who raised my siblings and me, with equal helpings of freedom, devotion, and a decidedly chipper eschewing of even the tiniest slice of negativity.

THE ELDEST CHILD and only daughter of Edwin and Helen Thomas, my mother grew up with a Navy dental officer father and my grandmother, a woman whose personality contrasted sharply with my mother's. From stories told over the years of my mom being sent to the coat closet with her hands tied together at the wrists for misbehaving in elementary school, I always gathered that she was a bit of a rebel. I never heard that she was nasty, spiteful, or mean, but conversations about my mom in her early years showcased a very active little girl who marched to a different drummer. When her first brother was born, two and a half years after she was, he represented yet another striking contrast to my mother. He barely spoke until he was three years old, and he could be relied upon to sit in a solitary corner of his playpen amusing himself with the same toys for hours on end.

With the addition of this little angel, there became a definite favorite in the house.

It wasn't my mother.

Growing up in a military home gave my mother a certain sense of adventure—and an understanding of what it was to stand by a husband whose career would uproot the family every few years or more. Perhaps she was drawn to that because that's what she knew. I know that she willingly signed up for that kind of life—and I also know that she was certainly overwhelmed with six very different children putting demands on her attention.

For all her embraceable qualities, my mother frequently had a hard time maintaining focus. It wasn't until the 1980s that people began talking about attention deficit disorder—and in reading through the telltale behaviors, our whole family agreed that Mom was the poster child. When my father's job demanded her focus in her role as his wife, she pulled herself together and was flawless. With us kids, however, it was almost as if dealing with any undesirable issues was just too much for her. She had trained as a nurse and worked as one just after the Korean war, so she was always attentive when one of us got injured enough to need mending. But she was much more comfortable allowing us our freedom—maybe because she wanted to give us something she didn't have growing up, or maybe because she didn't want to get involved in any of our drama.

The first time, for example, I went to my mother to lament

that one of my sisters was making my life miserable, she said, "Oh, just ignore her," in her singsong way with a flip of her hand.

I had wanted more from her, but I remember having the strong sense that I wasn't going to get it. If one of my siblings annoyed me, it was my job to deal with it, not hers. She wasn't unloving or detached, mind you; she simply put up a saccharine wall when any of us broached a topic better left brushed under the rug. With her often short attention span, my mother become a master at completely disregarding solvable problems; typical challenges were often ignored and put to the side as if they were invisible. This apparent aversion to tackling normal concerns perplexed me. Perhaps worse, with some of our more difficult family challenges, she looked the other way more readily than most mothers would have—particularly when it came to the sometimes abusive way my father handled things with us kids. She even went so far as to tell us that she couldn't understand why we had so many problems with each other when we had "the perfect family."

The ironic aspect of my mom's personality was that while she didn't want to discuss topics that unsettled her, she was remarkably open when it came to having other types of conversations or answering our questions. She was so easy to talk to, in fact—if she wasn't going in twelve directions—that I was never afraid to approach her the way I sometimes feared approaching my father. She may not have given me the answer I wanted, but she was always willing to listen.

One night, I remember waking up to odd noises coming from my parents' room. When I got up to investigate, my eyes grew wide: I saw what I can only call a passionate scene that I couldn't get my head around. The next day I mentioned it to Joyce.

"You're just realizing this now?" she said rolling her eyes. "They always do that."

I winced. "They *do?*"

"Well, *yeah,*" Joyce said, as if I should have known.

But I wanted a better explanation. So I found my mother in the kitchen and sidled up to her. "I saw what you and Dad were doing in your room last night," I whispered.

Clearly caught off guard, she turned abruptly toward me. She took in a little breath and smoothed her apron. "I'll talk with you about it later." Then she swooshed around me and left me standing there, slightly put off.

But the following Sunday, my parents sent the four younger kids to play in our finished basement and called Joyce and me to the kitchen table. I shifted uncomfortably in the squeaky vinyl chair as Mom and Dad told us precisely what men and women do to have a baby, which was far more detail than I wanted to hear.

"Now," my mother said firmly, finishing with a bang, "this can *only* happen when you're married."

No problem, I thought, *like I'm really ever going to do* that.

Just then, with my mother's final statement apparently signaling that the discussion was over, Joyce and my father bolted. But not me. I stayed behind to regale my mother with questions on how it all actually worked.

She sat quietly as she watched my enthusiasm get the better of me. Then, she simply patted my shoulder and said, "Just let nature take its course."

And that was pretty much the end of it.

For the time, discussing a taboo subject like sex in a Catholic household was avant garde. No doubt my mother dragged my father into it; I can't imagine he was a willing partner in the conversation. But no matter how it came about,

I considered myself lucky to have had their example—and I vowed to adopt their same attitude about sometimes awkward subjects and pass that ease on to my future children.

Several years later, when we had slid into the 1970s and times were continuing to change with the women's lib movement, the *marriage* part of my mother's admonition tripped me up a bit. Once again, I found my way to my mom.

"All the other girls are doing it," I told her, "and they're not married."

My mother paused only briefly. "Let me put it this way," she said, speaking to the teenage version of me like we were discussing the weather forecast, "would you ever buy a beautiful, shiny car that had an interior that was dirty and ripped up?"

With the greatest of ease, my mother had delivered my answer.

MORE THAN A decade later, after sex had long ceased being a curiosity and Bruce and I had three young boys of our own, I found myself being more and more introspective about my role as a mother. I loved how Mom had been so fun-loving with us growing up, despite her propensity for swimming in a pool of denial. While we were building our house in Ramona, we lived only a half mile from my parents, and Mom was the same fun, adventurous person she'd been with us. She had endless energy for sleepovers sacked out in sleeping bags in front of the fire, swim parties at her pool where Dad orchestrated races, hikes up the mountain behind their house, and hours of relaxation in the "children's room" where the grandkids were occasionally banished when all her adult children were home on weekends for dinner.

But I also couldn't help but reflect on my dad's temper and sometimes violent outbursts, and I realized how much they haunted me. Maybe because I was so focused on being the best mother to my sons, I was reminded far too often of the times my mother hadn't been there for her children when we were at our most defenseless.

On one of her visits, when it was just the two of us still up one night, I was tidying up the kitchen while she chattered on and on as she usually did. Her excessive talking was something we often laughed about; over the years, it had become so wearing that we kids jokingly named it her "talking problem." She would actually roll her eyes if one of us asked for her attention because she knew that meant she'd have to be quiet for a minute. This time, in place of asking, I waited until she stopped to take a breath and jumped right in.

"Mom, I want to ask you an uncomfortable question. Are you up for that?"

She looked toward me, a bit startled. "I guess so."

I took a cleansing breath. "I've had some hard feelings, Mom. It's not fair for you to wonder why I'm quiet at times."

She looked confused.

I walked over to where she sat warming herself next to the pot-bellied stove. I knew my words might hurt, but I also hoped they might be healing.

"Mom," I said gently, "why did you let Dad get away with his tirades directed at us? We were scared to death. I remember one time running to you for comfort while he wreaked havoc downstairs on the kids. You half-heartedly said, 'It's not the end of the world.'"

Her speechlessness was uncharacteristic. She sat for what seemed like forever as I stood silently next to her. Finally, she said, "I think times were different then. There wasn't the awareness there is now about things like that. I knew it would be over with soon and figured you kids would forget." Her voice lowered to a near whisper. "Breathing life into it would peg me against your father, and that would have been awful."

Mom had always warned us not to "breathe life" into whatever negativity we faced. While no one could accuse her of not walking her talk, her detachment during those times did have some intense consequences for us kids.

I stared at my mother. It was in that moment that I realized this strong, capable woman who was all things to all people was also glaringly human. For some self-preserving reason, she avoided trouble in the face of fear, particularly when it came to my father.

She looked up at me. "If I could go back," she said sincerely, "I'd do things differently."

My shoulders fell with an exhale and my face melted into a warm smile. Instantly, I saw my mother at her most vulnerable, and therefore most magical, and I felt flooded with love for her in a way I never had before. The pain in my heart was replaced with the tenderness a mother feels for her child—only that night our roles were reversed. I saw my mother as my child, one who deserved to have my resentment turn into compassion. As my long-held burden faded away, I saw my mother radiant in the face of her admission: it had taken a great deal of courage to be genuine with me, whether she felt she was owning up to failure or acknowledging what she viewed as her own terror from those days. Instead of putting herself between us and that terror, she had turned a blind eye and never mentioned it again—until now.

That night was huge for both of us. My heart wasn't only lighter, it was more bonded to hers that it ever had been.

But my mother still carried a deep, dark secret, one that would take a few more years to be brought into the light.

❧

AFTER ALL OF us were grown and had moved away from home, my mom went back to school to become a certified alcohol and drug counselor (CADC). In a way I could only admire, she declared it her way of "helping others when she couldn't help her own son." The program involved complete self-reflection, requiring her to take copious notes of her life events. Though it wasn't easy for her, she was very open with all of us about it. Most curious of all was my dad, who transcribed all of her journaling.

One evening, while typing her day's scribblings, Dad was stopped cold. Over and over, he read the new paragraphs in complete disbelief. After pausing for a time to absorb the shock, he typed the notes up as promised, but he found it difficult to shake what my mother had divulged.

During the years her father was aboard the naval hospital ship, when my mother was a teenager, a couple who lived down the road invited them over every Sunday for dinner. They lived on a rural piece of property with a barn and chicken coop, and every time her family visited, the man would take my mother out to the barn "to see the animals." Only that wasn't his motivation. He had used the trust that he and his wife built with my mother's parents to whisk their daughter away to a secluded place where he could repeatedly molest her.

My mother never told anyone about these weekly sessions of sexual abuse, and my grandparents, I suspect, never imagined that anything inappropriate was going on during these visits. I could accuse my grandmother of not being tapped in to her child enough to know something terrible was happening to her, but I can't know that for sure. I also don't know if Mom ever conveyed not wanting to go to the neighbors' house for dinner—hopeful her mother would read between the lines—and her pleas fell on deaf ears. All I know is that my mother often expressed how much she hated being a teenager. She was so desperate, in fact, to get out of her house that after her junior year in high school, she researched boarding schools and found the perfect one in North Carolina. She secretly applied and was accepted, then begged her parents to let her go.

Securing her parents' permission—at an age when most teens would never want to be the new girl in school—my mother packed her bags, moved to a foreign place, and enrolled as an incoming senior. I was always amazed by how she spoke of that time with such happiness and the fondest of memories. But after my father confided in us what my mother had revealed in her journaling, I finally understood. She had endured enough as a teenager, and she was done. By taking her life into her own hands and forging her own path, she enabled herself to shine; the photos and stories of her during that period reflect a beautiful, self-assured, spunky young girl having the time of her life.

Until then, I never knew why but often thought there was something more to this loving, happy, spirited woman who was my mother, a woman who saw only what she wanted to see. I couldn't understand why she so often turned the other cheek when my dad was angry or when one of us was disrespectful. Talking back was absolutely not allowed within earshot of my dad, yet with Mom it was different; we got away with being the emotionally charged bunch we were and saying what we wanted. She had a way of simply "taking it" that was peculiar. Now, I couldn't help but wonder if she had not only been threatened by the pedophile if she ever breathed a word, but that she internalized from her experiences with him that when she hurt, she wasn't worth fighting for, that she somehow didn't merit the respect she deserved. I had often wished my mother could have been more to us in some ways, but in receiving this news, I softened. The thought of her being hurt by this man destroyed me, and I couldn't get to her fast enough.

When I arrived at her house, I was emotionally charged. Rushing to her, I took her hand. She looked at me alarmed.

"Dad told me how you were sexually abused as a young girl. I'm so sad about it, Mom. I just wanted you to know I know and that I'm so sorry." I wiped tears from my face as she sat stoically. "I don't know how you've stood it all these years. If you ever want to talk about it, I'm here for you."

I grew quiet and looked for clues on my mother's face that might convey what she was feeling. But instead of the big smile and talkativeness she met most situations with, there was no emotion at all.

After a brief silence, she said, "Yes, I was sexually abused for a long time. Uncle Bob had a friend and we went every Sunday for dinner at their house." She looked down at her hands that lay gently overlapped. "At some point after dinner the father would beckon me to go for a walk and see the chickens. I knew what I was in for as he led me to the barn. He did what he always did, and when it was over we'd walk back to the house like nothing happened."

I offered her more comforting words from my heart. Then, as I looked into her expressionless eyes, it all coalesced for me: my mother's intense desire to be happy was rooted somehow in this horrible time in her life—and if maintaining this happiness meant frequently overlooking obvious unrest within our family, then so be it. Once she made up her mind to be in charge of her own contentment, she didn't waver. This was why she was completely dismissive of certain topics and willing to talk about others. If she could handle it, the conversation was open; if she couldn't, it was immediately met with "Oh, it'll be fine," or "Oh, you'll handle it," or "Oh, just ignore it."

Not a tear fell from my mother's eyes—but she never did cry over sad events, only over sentimental ones. Had crying as a child garnered her punishment, or perhaps even a complete lack of sympathy? If so, then maybe she determined early on that crying over anything upsetting had no payoff, and therefore turned those emotions off for good. Either way, I now faced a woman who had harbored great distress—one she had skillfully stuffed—since she was a girl, and I once again felt our bond grow to a new level.

IN THE LATE 1990s, my parents set out on a 400-mile hiking trip on the Appalachian trail. They had spent an entire year training for it, and after being gone for weeks, they arrived home to an exuberant crowd of family at Lindbergh Field with welcome signs and balloons. I was amazed at how good they looked and how high their spirits were. Fit and tan, they were full of excitement to share their tales in the wild.

Before nightfall, they gathered all of us together for an announcement.

"We've decided to embark on another adventure," Dad said with enthusiasm.

I was taken aback. I had made a difficult decision to tell my parents some disturbing news during one of our brief phone calls while they were away, and I expected them to still be at odds with what they came home to, not making plans for another trip. One of my sisters had become fully engulfed in alcohol addiction, and although it was bad before they left, it had escalated to an even more dangerous level while they were gone. Fearing for her life, Bruce and I had checked on her regularly in my parents' guest house where she was living. She pleaded with me to just leave her alone, but I couldn't. The day I found a burning cigarette on the rug was the day I decided I couldn't worry any longer about ruining my parents' vacation with bad news.

Now, here my dad was, poised to share plans with us for their next adventure.

"While we were in North Carolina on a brief stint off the trail," he said, "we bought a house in Wake Forest."

Stunned silence filled the room. I glanced around at my siblings and saw that we all had the same looks on our faces, as if we'd just been punched in the stomach.

For years, they had lived near us in Southern California. But while they loved their grandchildren and spending time with us, they had always been East Coast people at heart. Many of their friends and some family members were there, and they had decided it was time for them to make the move.

Besides being shocked and devastated, I couldn't believe they would choose to move now of all times, when one of their daughters was so impaired.

I pulled my parents aside and implored them to talk to a counselor to see if there was anything they could do to help my sister. They acquiesced, but I could tell that neither of them thought there was much hope.

True to their word, they did consult with the counselor I recommended. But succumbing to a feeling of helplessness, they ultimately agreed that they couldn't commit to the tough love necessary to be of any help.

Within weeks, their house was sold, the moving van was packed, and they were gone.

The boys and their cousins had all been so little when Grama and Grampa moved to Ramona in 1986, it was almost as if they didn't know life without them. I felt sad, angry, and an overwhelming sense of abandonment over their decision, but I hid my disappointment and focused on comforting my children, nieces, and nephews. My siblings were equally incensed by our parents' abrupt departure, refusing to go visit them. I, too, stewed in my stubbornness and held out for nearly a year before flying my family of five to North Carolina.

It wasn't until a year or two later that my dear friend, Erica, passed on something her mother Mikey expressed when they were discussing my parents' leaving.

"They raised their family," Mikey said. "They shouldn't feel obligated to suffer through their adult children's mistakes. They're at a point where they should be enjoying their retirement."

Until then, I had only seen it from a child's perspective, not from theirs. It was wonderful to spend so much time with them when they became grandparents, but I had never considered that they might have dreams of their own. Once I realized how self-centered we all had been, I felt my first measure of peace since they'd told us they were leaving.

MOM AND DAD spent many summers visiting California. Bruce and I relished our time with them at our country home, sitting by the pool while my mom swam with the kids. When they weren't staying with us, we went to Joyce's house where we spent days at the beach. It was during those visits that I bobbed around in the chilly Pacific with my mom. Though I wasn't a water baby, I inherited my love of cold water from her, and she looked forward to our time in the waves together. Being buoyed by the ocean calmed her down to the point where our conversations were slow and easy. I remember looking at her and noticing that her eyes were as ice blue as the cloudless sky and her smile more glorious than the majestic bluffs to the east of the shoreline. We'd stay until our shivering brought us back to the beach to bask in the warming sun.

During those times, I treasured finding a way to be with my mom that was pure connection. Being one of so many kids had made it difficult to command my mother's attention for me alone, but swaying and drifting out there on the ocean like that, just the two of us, was the discovery of the truest love a girl could share with her mother.

IN OCTOBER OF 2008, after the accident had sent my dad into the last stage of his life, my mother didn't come out for Bruce's funeral. I was surprised that I was fine without her at such a horrible time, but I realized what I did have: the secure feeling of knowing it wasn't her presence that grounded me, it was her love. But when we lost Patrick, even though my dad had passed away only eight days prior, Mom flew out with my sister, Carol, and her daughter, Maggie—and all that security I thought I had won without her presence was enhanced by her being there. She slept with me in my bed, and when I'd hear her stir in the morning, I'd go downstairs and get coffee for us. When I returned, she'd be sitting up waiting for me. Although she didn't allow herself to cry, she was raw in a way I'd never seen her.

I would climb with our cups onto the bed, where the stillness of our shared pain filled the room that had been Bruce's and mine so little time ago. I would cry my heart out for my son while she quietly listened. After unleashing my impenetrable pain, we would sit in silence for a little while, and then she would start talking about my dad. Sadness was not an emotion my mother had ever willingly expressed, but my parents' love was so deep, their connection so strong, that we struggled for breath in it together, mother and daughter, as we shared our mutual losses and the irreparable heartbreaks they had left in their wake.

Growing up Catholic, it was customary to hang rosaries from the bedpost. They represented safety and soothing, and they were in easy reach before we slept or when we awoke in the morning. Though by then I was no longer a practicing Catholic, I still derived comfort from what those beads symbolized.

One morning, my mom reached for mine and I put my hand up. "You pray the rosary for both of us," I said. "I'll meditate for us instead."

She raised her eyebrows a hint and we both laughed.

Some things do change. The rest—the things Mom couldn't feel comfortable with—she simply didn't breathe life into. It was easier to accept that way.

AS THAT DARKEST of winters progressed, my mother returned to North Carolina, to the circle of friends and family who would see her through life without her husband. I missed her deeply, but I knew she couldn't stay forever. And I knew I needed to learn for myself how to move forward without my own husband and son.

❧

ON FEBRUARY 3, 2009, I was sitting at my desk when I realized Mom hadn't called yet. It would have been Bruce's and my thirty-year anniversary, and she was always the first to call on a special occasion. Concerned but not alarmed, I resumed writing in my journal.

Less than an hour later, I received an odd call from the funeral home I'd used for Bruce and Patrick. They told me they had a number for a hospital by my mom's house in Wake Forest and that I needed to call.

I was confused. "What's this about? Is my mom okay?"

The woman told me that the police had found my mother in her car. "She was conscious but she must have suffered a stroke," she said. "Her car was found in a ditch."

I panicked. "A ditch? Oh my God." Then confusion. "But I don't understand . . . how are *you* aware of all this?"

"I know it's a lot to process," she said. "There was a business card in your mom's purse of an old friend, an attorney in California she'd gotten reacquainted with at Patrick's funeral. It was all the police had to go on." She went on to explain that they called this man for clues as to who this person they'd found might be. He couldn't remember my married name, but he did remember the name of the funeral home. When he contacted them, it wasn't hard to pinpoint who I was when he recounted the family that had two losses to suicide within eight weeks. That's when I got the call that my mom was severely impaired from a hemorraghic stroke and was in the ICU.

I flew to North Carolina immediately. When I saw her lying in her hospital bed, she looked as if losing my dad had simply been too much for her. She had held fast to her optimism for decades, refusing to allow negativity into her circle if she could help it, but this loss was something she had no control over.

I took her hand in mine and told her everything would be okay. As nurses, we both knew too well what she was up against. Her speech had been affected, so she couldn't respond, but that wasn't unusual in the days following a stroke.

I had no idea that aside from rare occasions when she would eke out an "I love you," my mother, whom we had teased—and begrudgingly at times tolerated—for years about her incessant talking, would never really speak again.

THOUGH MY MOTHER could eat and amble about with a walker, her spirit was clearly dampened. Remarkably, we found a way to communicate over the phone, with me talking and her making sounds in response that I grew to understand. During my predawn trips to the hospital for work, I'd call her as she was getting up on Eastern time and describe the breathtaking sunrises I was driving toward. Sometimes I did the same during sunsets, remembering fondly how she'd pull over when we were kids if the sunset was spectacular. I had done the same with my own family: when the sun in Ramona settled into the distant ocean, I'd yell to my brood and they'd all come running.

One day, we were chatting (well, I was chatting), and I remarked that most difficult things had a silver lining.

"You know, Mom," I said, "as tragic as it was that the stroke deprived you of your speech, I feel like I finally get my chance to lead the conversation."

At that, she broke out laughing and I laughed right along with her.

✆

OVER THE NEXT five years, we witnessed the bright light that was my mother dimming a little more each time during our frequent visits to North Carolina. She didn't have music playing nonstop anymore. The mail on her desk was piled high. She sat for long periods on the couch just staring. On occasion, she'd lie down for a totally uncharacteristic nap. It also weighed on me heavily that I'd had so little time to talk to her between Bruce's dying and her stroke. After being a person I could always go to, her speechlessness meant that I had lost my chance to have a deep conversation with her about how I would rebuild my life. With Dad gone too, I truly felt on my own in how to move forward. It didn't matter that I had five decades of life experience to claim as mine. I still longed for the balm of my parents' guidance, in whatever way they would have been willing to offer it.

One of the things I relied upon in my healing journey was the ritual of writing in my journal. It was here that I could talk to God, express my emotions, and document my fears and hopes. It was also the place where I sometimes found inspiration to write poetry.

On one balmy, overcast day that mirrored me inside and out during one of my visits to North Carolina, these words tumbled out to my mom.

The golden light of early morning
Glistened through the pine trees
Setting the mood for the stillness that surrounded us.
We sat quietly
No more words for you
Thinking our thoughts

Sharing the sacred space of you and me.
As I looked at your sadness
No emotion in your face
No tears.
It was then my tears began to fall
Big drops followed bigger ones
Splashing on your nightgown I had borrowed.
The sadness in your face
Was the sort of sadness life gives
When you can't go back again.
You, trapped in your powerlessness
To help me in my sorrow,
Me, not missing your unspoken thoughts
Of a bigger emotion I couldn't miss—
Your broken heart for your husband
For your son-in-law
For your young grandson
And for your daughter.
You had no tears
And I didn't expect them
Instead I remembered the vibrant home we had
And your smile that covered all heartaches then
Your optimism that worked miracles
Gone forever.
Still I couldn't miss the magic
As the glow from a new day
Shined gently behind your back,
Of the life we now shared and the void in our hearts
For them nearly palpable.
I embraced this wordless time
When the common ground we shared
Felt suddenly as precious

As the memories of times gone by,
When our home then was full
With talking and laughing
And our hearts were whole
And minutes like this with you were stolen and treasured.
I think of the places life takes us
In spite of our efforts:
"It is what it is, right, Mom?"
I want to say.
We must navigate through it
Together
Surrounded and comforted
By the golden light of early morning
Glistening through the pine trees
Setting the mood for the stillness.

NEARLY FIVE YEARS to the day, sometime in mid-February, Carol called to say that Mom had had another massive stroke. She was in the hospital with no swallow reflex and couldn't move the entire left side of her body. Bedridden and fed by a tube, she wasn't expected to last very long. And in that state, all of us prayed for God to take her quickly.

The next day, my sister held the phone up to my mother's ear so that I could speak to her.

"Mom, it's Mary," I said softly. "I want you to go if you're ready. We will all be fine. You can be with Dad and Patrick and Bruce. They're waiting for you." She made a small sound as my heart swelled. I didn't cry. Instead I was filled with the sense that this was what my mom's long life had come to, and that she deserved peace and encouragement. "You were the best mother anyone could ever have hoped for," I told her. "I love you with all my heart."

With that, Carol took the phone and said she had to go.

❧

THE NEXT MORNING, around five a.m., the phone rang. It was my sister.

"Is Mom gone?" I asked.

"Yes," Carol said tearfully. "She died a few minutes ago."

I hung up the phone and sat in the stillness of the predawn morning. Even though I knew my mother's dying was imminent, I felt stunned. I couldn't help but think how it hadn't been an easy road for her with her high level of energy, her inability to focus, and her long-suppressed sexual trauma. Yet my blonde-haired, blue-eyed spitfire of a mother had embraced a carefreeness atypical of a harried mother of six. With one of the kindest, most loving hearts, my mother became an unflappable and selfless wife, mom, and friend to many. From somewhere deep inside her, she seemed to have a clear understanding of what hadn't worked in her life, so she turned the parts she could into beautiful personality traits. What she couldn't—or possibly chose not to—take on and change became the signature qualities, whether disconcerting or endearing, of the loving, caring, giving person who raised me.

Reflecting on this resilient woman I had always loved deeply, the one my friends had adored and often wished was their own mother, I felt an overwhelming sense of calm. Then, almost like a reflex, I spoke softly into the darkness. "I'm happy for you, Mom. I'm so happy for you."

a

wedding

pierre

*T*HE FIRST YEAR AFTER BRUCE DIED, APART FROM being there for my sons, I preferred living in virtual isolation. Almost every day, I would walk for miles and miles on the beach near where I lived, and I only took calls and visited with loved ones and friends when I felt I could handle it. Eventually, on certain days, I would bring myself to shower and dress and go to Starbucks or on a brief shopping trip. Being out in stores again allowed me to feel the first sparks of what a new home would be like and what I would fill it with, thoughts that began to pull me out into the world once again. But what I couldn't imagine was dating someone new. Though I felt no loyalty to Bruce in that way—which surprised me after being married nearly thirty years—I actually confided to my niece, Rachel, that I had possibly enjoyed my last days of intimacy. From the look on her sweet, twenty-one-year-old face, I could see that I had stepped over the comfort line with that one.

But over time, after thoughts of Bruce's leaving had returned to me over and over, I concluded that there was nothing for me to be loyal to when it came to my husband. Bruce was gone by his own choice—and I believed I had every right to have love again in my life with a man. Once I realized that, I knew romantic love was a path I was willing to go down again someday. I just wondered when I'd ever feel it in my heart.

For the time being, I remained pretty much in my own

safe bubble of a world. Among my saving graces were my work friends, with whom I relished numerous cups of coffee, and whose love, caring, and acceptance kept me uplifted. But at some point, I realized I couldn't lean on them indefinitely. In a way, it reminded me of when I lived in Pacific Beach as an eighteen-year-old on her own for the first time, reliant on a handful of work friends to help me acclimate to my new life. Back then, I had experienced more solitude than I was used to having grown up in our boisterous family, but I had lived on the pride of persevering on my own and building a nice life for myself. And now, I was feeling that same sense of solitude, that same necessity to reinvent myself. In reality, I was Mary Odgers—widow; mother of three sons, one deceased; working full-time as a nurse because I had to; praying every day I wouldn't be so sad. I wasn't quite sure how to be Mary Odgers, single mother of two grown sons, happily working full-time because I wanted to, waking up every day confident in myself and in moving forward.

When I determined I was as ready as I thought I would ever be, I was only up for casual meetings for coffee; back then, I couldn't imagine having appetite enough to go out to dinner. Other men I met by chance on runs, on hikes up Mt. Woodson, or during walks on the beach. These men gave me the gift of being noticed, but I only went out more than once with one man—the rest I hoped would let me off the hook before inviting me to go somewhere I didn't feel like going. They were all nice enough, and though I couldn't imagine I'd lost all interest in intimacy, I never felt anything with these men in return, and I didn't want to invest my time in seeing if the feelings would grow.

But the Universe has a way of guiding us toward what our heart needs and desires, even when that picture isn't clear for us. The individual occurrences may seem unlinked while in the moment, but when viewed in sequence, they bring to light a truly magical and serendipitous series of events.

ONE AFTERNOON, on the way back from one of my walks, I grabbed the mail from the box and shuffled through it. A couple of bills, our local *Del Mar Times*, some junk . . . and something I'd been expecting but was still shocked to see: the life insurance check for Bruce. I went inside and lowered myself onto the couch. I carefully opened the envelope and stared at the check. The amount was more than I'd ever dreamed of or even wanted, and I couldn't help but think about the irony of receiving money in the face of tremendous loss, as if it were some measure of compensation. But I was also grateful to Bruce, deeply grateful that despite everything, he had looked out for us in this way.

Feeling overwhelmed by the check and all the things it signified, I slid it back into the envelope and laid it on the table. Wanting a momentary distraction, I picked up the newspaper and was paging through it when I spotted the face of an old friend. I'd heard he had gone into real estate nearby, but our paths hadn't crossed in over thirty years and I doubted he'd remember me. Still, I took a chance. I called and left a message using my maiden name. Within a day, we had reconnected and were out looking at houses.

John was full of enthusiasm and words of wisdom for me. "You know, Mary," he said, "I've dealt with clients for years in this area. You're in a lucky position for a woman in her fifties. You're financially free and can do whatever you want." I raised my eyebrows and nodded slightly, not having considered that. "This part of the county is full of women your age with no husbands, little money, and searching for someone to take care of them. But you . . . you *can* be and *should* be selective. Take your time. You owe it to yourself and your family to be happy again."

John's words settled into me like a ray of sun on a chilly day. I suddenly saw myself as having something to offer instead of needing something from someone else. I *was* self-sufficient, and that meant I was in the driver's seat of life. I had an excellent job, two wonderful sons, and money enough to feel secure. And now with John's help, I was certain I'd find a new house soon. After all the tragedy I'd been through, it was the first inkling I'd had in more than two years that I was lucky.

IN A RELATIVELY brief period of time, John found a condo I loved in Solana Beach that was only a three-minute walk to the waves of the Pacific. The place needed some work, but I now had the means to remodel it to my liking when I was ready. I signed all the paperwork, and within months of escrow closing, I had moved in and begun rebuilding my life as a single woman.

I clearly remember that on my first weekend there, my phone didn't ring once. The silence was glaring, but within that pocket of quietude, I also felt a strong sense that my life was moving on. I wasn't merely surviving, I was taking deliberate steps forward. Somehow, after many months of feeling nearly nothing but pain and sadness, I felt a spirit rise up in me that carried possibilities for the future. I didn't have a specific vision; I just knew good things were on their way.

Shortly afterward, I began the remodel of the condo—which meant moving in with my sister for three months. I had finally broken down and bought a couch, a table, and a bed, and one day at work, I wondered out loud where I would store them. One of the doctors I'd known for years, though not well, overheard me and offered his extra garage.

"That would be great!" I said with sincere gratitude.

Dr. Lotzof and I had rarely spoken to each other at the hospital before that. But he was one of our most respected anesthesiologists, and it had always been a bright light in my day when I'd see him. We didn't have much of a connection, and he always seemed to be in a hurry, but he was a nice, upbeat sort of man. When he'd wheel a patient into the recovery room where I was working, I might say, "Oh, Dr. Lotzof . . . now I know it's going to be a great day!"

On one particular day back in 2007, I was checking on the patient I was soon to get in the recovery room—his patient—when the subject of fiftieth birthdays came up. I told him about the catered party under a big white tent my family had just put on for me in August, and he told me he was going to his native South Africa for his that September. He was nice and chatty and clearly loved wild animals, which I found fascinating.

Now, two years later, a lot had transpired in my life, and everyone at the hospital had been incredibly loving and kind to me. Dr. Lotzof had never said anything to me directly about Bruce's and Patrick's deaths, but the anesthesiology group had been the first to send flowers after Bruce died. I didn't know if Dr. Lotzof's offer to store my furniture was one made as a gesture to help a grieving woman, or if he was simply a nice person in that way. But within a few days, Matt and I were driving my furniture to his house—a beautiful 6,000-square-foot home with a yard like the Garden of Eden. He welcomed us as friends and shared that he was divorced and lived alone with his twelve-year-old son, Elan, who was having his bar mitzvah soon. He said they would be welcoming visitors from around the world, and I told him he could use my furniture if he needed it for his extra guests. As he took me up on his offer, I couldn't believe my luck that he had overheard me mumbling about my storage dilemma that day and I was now standing across from him, immensely enjoying our naturally flowing conversation.

From that day on we shared a common comfort zone. He asked me to call him by his first name, Pierre, and we met for coffee when his schedule allowed. When he returned from yet another trip to South Africa, I was touched to be the first phone call he made. Could we meet for coffee? he wanted to know. I agreed enthusiastically.

As Pierre happily talked about his visit abroad, I felt pangs of something I hadn't felt in a long time: a certain brand of warmth emanating from him that felt like interest in me.

"I went on a blind date in South Africa," he told me matter-of-factly. He waited a beat before saying, "It wasn't a match."

I smiled in spite of myself, realizing I felt something for him and hoped our regular rendezvous wouldn't end.

"Meeting this girl got me thinking." He took a sip of his coffee. "I've decided I'm going to date only younger women from now on."

My heart sank. After discussing our birthdays a couple years prior, he knew I was barely two months older than he was. But I figured that his blind date was perhaps a much younger woman, and though it hadn't worked out, she sparked something in him that made him want to date women who weren't his age. I was disappointed that I apparently wasn't a candidate for his dating pool, but I was also grateful to feel a part of my old self, the self that was human and capable of feeling something magical again.

"Good luck with that," I replied with a lighthearted laugh.

He nodded and laughed too. "Thanks."

I left shortly after that with mixed feelings—a light feeling in my heart laced with the slightest tinge of dismay. But before I pulled into my sister's driveway, he called.

"Just wanted to say thanks for the nice time," he said.

Refusing to get caught up in mixed messages from him, I took him for one of those people who made impulsive phone calls to simply share fleeting thoughts. I didn't mind, but I did admonish myself to keep our connection straight in my own head. He had definitely shown interest in me, so I could have easily believed he liked me as more than a friend. But since he'd made himself clear that he had other ideas for his single life, I couldn't allow myself to go there.

Pierre and I continued to meet for the occasional coffee after a shift, and I continued to be friendly yet detached. But on one particular evening, I noticed him squirming a little in his chair. He was inclined to do that when our conversations occasionally turned serious, but this time, he said he wanted to ask me something.

"Sure. Go ahead." I picked up my cup and peered at him over the rim.

"Would you come to the hospital gala with me?" His eyes darted downward then back up to me. "I don't know if it's right for me to ask you, but I figured you wouldn't hold it against me even if you didn't want to go."

So much for the younger women.

I couldn't deny that I wanted more with this man, but I also couldn't ignore the feeling in my stomach: elation and dread made for a disconcerting mixture. I set my cup down. Heeding my usual reluctance to rush into things, I said, "Can I take a little time to think about it? I have to admit, I feel a little confused."

"Of course," he said. "I'll call you tomorrow."

The second I got into my car, I called Maripat.

"I just got asked out on a date!" I squealed with the excitement of a teenager.

"You're not going are you?" she blurted out.

Taken aback by the disapproving way her response landed on my ears, I countered, "That's not the point! I've just been asked out on a date!"

But Maripat didn't join me in my excitement. By the end of our call, she had convinced me that it was a bad idea, not because Pierre wasn't a potentially good guy, but because I wasn't ready for more than casual meetings, she didn't want me getting hurt, enjoying good company should have no pretense tied to it . . . the list went on.

I put a lot of stock in what Maripat thought, especially with my being so vulnerable at the time, but I also didn't like her telling me to take my time with that part of my life. If I didn't feel ready, I felt no need to push it. I'd been on plenty of dates and been asked out a second time, but this was different. Pierre's invitation hit me in a place that desired affirmation; I was thrilled that he wanted me to attend the gala with him. And there was something else: Pierre hadn't dwelled on my tragedy as so many others had, albeit lovingly. Some of the other men I'd gone out with had expressed wanting to help me through my difficult time—but "help" isn't what I wanted. I longed for a companion to share my life with, not to be someone's rescue project. Until then, Pierre was the only man who hadn't made it his mission to help me in some way. His manner could have been taken as insensitive, but for me, it felt perfect. I had often uttered a silent prayer before a date: "Just be a bright light in my dull days. Don't participate in the loss." But understandably, this was a tall order for most people. If they didn't acknowledge or talk about my grief, they felt they were being unsympathetic. But Pierre had done the best job yet of answering that prayer. He had been properly speechless and caring when it was appropriate, but mostly he didn't let his rather active, distractible mind rest too long on any one thing, specifically my troubles.

It was barely eight a.m. the next day when my phone rang and I saw the 858 number I was hoping for.

"Have you made your mind up yet?"

I laughed at his transparency and his lack of desire to hide it.

"I have," I said. "And . . . my answer is no, not this time. I'm just not ready."

He was quiet.

"I'm so happy you asked, though," I added with a smile. "Promise me you'll ask me next year."

THE NEXT TIME I saw Pierre, a few days later, he had already secured another date for the gala. When he told me, I felt the telltale signs of sliding down a slippery slope of attachment: heart sinking, a twinge of disappointment. But after the gala, he confided that the event was just okay and the date was "nice." Though I wasn't preoccupied with thoughts of him liking her enough to see her again, I admit I did wonder. It took no time at all for us to start spending more time together.

A couple months into our more frequent outings, I decided it was time for Pierre and me to have a serious talk. I willingly embraced my vulnerability and somehow trusted in the possibilities that were before me. Setting the mood with soft music and candlelight, I felt for the first time in a long time that loss was not final, that love and hope were possible and that my life could go on to be beautiful. I was ready to see if all this would apply to Pierre.

We sat down at the dining room table. "So," I ventured bravely, "what do you see for us and our future?"

"What do you mean?" he asked coyly, as if he'd been expecting this conversation.

I sat up a little straighter. "I guess I'm looking to define our relationship a little. We obviously like each other. I wonder what thoughts and parameters you want to put around it."

He hesitated only briefly. "No thoughts at all, and as for parameters . . ." His voice trailed off, but not for long. "I'm happy with the way things are. I don't feel a need to qualify it in any way. We have a good thing and I want more of it."

I took a deep breath. *If only it was as simple for me as it is for you*, I thought.

"I agree," I said, shifting a little. "I've never felt a need to talk about us seeing other people, but I feel like it's time—for me anyway—to suggest that we agree to have it be . . . just you and me."

I felt myself floundering and a sense that my words were floating past him instead of being absorbed. He wasn't looking directly at me and his sudden restlessness spoke volumes.

"Mary," he finally said, "let's not ruin a good thing. I love our relationship just the way it is . . . and no, I haven't dated anyone else. But I want to leave myself open. I was married for fifteen years. I don't want to get back into that scene right away. I want to be free from that . . . but I want you to be a part of my life."

In the past two years, circumstances had robbed me of any sense of control or power in my life. But now, though his words planted a sense of disappointment in me, I also felt an overriding feeling of freedom. I could make the choice that was right for me, decide if *Pierre* was right for me. It had been a long time since I felt empowered. Even if things didn't work out between us, I was remarkably ready to stand strong on my own two feet.

"So you want to see me and other women too?" I asked, trying not to sound bothered.

He gave a slight shrug, as if to say, "Well, yes."

I pursed my lips gently. "I have to tell you, I'm overjoyed by your honesty . . . but I can't imagine that for me. I can't agree to what you're offering . . . and I wouldn't be happy dating people outside of you. It's just not me."

He looked slightly surprised—taken aback, or perhaps admiring my resoluteness.

"You obviously feel certain about your desires and you should pursue them," I continued. "But there's no way I can ignore what my heart wants. I was married for thirty years and I want another relationship in my life—but only one. I don't mind meeting other people until I've found the right one." I looked away for a moment then zeroed in on his eyes. "I was willing to consider that I may have lucked out and found the right one immediately. I've hoped it was you."

His eyes and face showed no definitive expression other than I had his full attention.

"Do you think I'm shallow?" he finally said.

"Yes!" I blurted, and we both burst out laughing.

I patted his hand. "Maybe I could be a little bit more that way," I offered, "but I'm just not light about these things. I *am* feeling very lucky right now, though."

"Lucky?" he said, sounding confused. "In what way?"

"I'm impressed that we figured this out early in our relationship. And I'm really happy we're being honest about what we want. I love that part of you." I went on to tell him that I knew it could have played out differently, that I was certainly no expert at romance, having been in a relationship since I was nineteen and married at twenty-one. "The fact that we're so clear in each of our positions is such a gift. You deserve to have the life you want . . . and I do too. Maybe someday we'll see it the same. But for now, I just hope we find our way back to each other if things change for you."

I had been jabbering on with the enthusiasm of someone who felt like she won a coveted prize—and that I accepted my time with the prize was coming to a possible end. I had met a wonderful man who took my mind from self-centeredness and sorrow to happiness. I had begun to laugh again. Even when Pierre didn't mean to be funny, he entertained me. The way he saw things, the comments he made, the quick-wittedness—it was all refreshingly authentic. I adored it and *him*. He had been my gift for a time and now I was on to the next chapter. I stood up.

He looked at me perplexed. "So . . . I should leave?"

"I think it's best," I said, heading for the door.

He rose slowly. "You really mean it . . . starting now. I'm so surprised. We have such a good thing." He continued shaking his head and having his one-sided conversation as I grabbed his car key and phone and followed him out to his car.

He turned to face me.

"This isn't easy for me," I admitted. "But the future won't be easy if we don't honor what we both want."

He nodded, seeming to consider I was right.

"Of course I feel sad at the thought of not being in contact with you, but that will fade in time." My resolve surprised us both, but I didn't show it from my end. "I think it's best if we just let things cool off a little. We probably shouldn't talk on the phone or get together casually until this sinks in, okay? My heart won't change anytime soon . . . and I won't be able to disconnect from you if we stay in constant contact."

Pierre took in a breath and said he agreed.

"Oh," I added, "if you change your mind, let me know immediately."

I thought he might laugh, but instead he got into his car. Before he closed the door, I heard him say, "I may be making the biggest mistake of my life."

Whether or not he meant for me to hear that, I held strong to steadfast Mary and sent him off with one last remark.

"Hopefully I'll be available if you find that to be true and decide to come back with a different mindset."

With that, I pivoted and walked up the front stairs.

Less than ten minutes later, my phone rang.

"I forgot my pager. I'm heading back."

I was waiting outside when he pulled up. Pointing to the heavens, I said, "I'm positive this is a sign. Hurry up and change your mind!"

He merely shook his head and laughed.

FOR THE NEXT couple weeks, Pierre broke our agreement not to be in touch. He called intermittently—and each time my heart leapt with joy when I saw his name. We'd chat a little and then I'd ask him if he wanted to alter his decision on us seeing each other, that my feelings for him hadn't changed. "No," he'd say, a barely discernible edge in his voice.

"Have you been dating?" I'd push.

"No, I have no motivation. You?"

"No. No one compares to you."

He'd chuckle. I couldn't tell if he was flattered or annoyed, but that was how we'd end most of our calls. Though I didn't want to cave to my emotions, I found myself crying each time we hung up. It was killing me that he would call and be so sweet and playful, igniting this newfound joy in me, yet not want to see me exclusively. Finally, frustrated with this repeated scenario, I asked him to please not call me anymore.

The next morning on my way to the hospital, I received a text from him. I read it and promptly deleted it. When I arrived in the unit, he was wheeling in a patient from the OR. "Hey, you didn't answer my text," he whispered as he breezed by.

I crossed my arms over my chest. "And I won't."

"That's not in the rules," he shot back.

"Rules? I make the rules now," I said with conviction.

The truth was that despite my frustration with our cat and mouse routine, I had the comforting realization that no matter what might come of my connection with Pierre, he had been a catalyst for opening me up to move forward in my life in a way I hadn't expected—and for that, I was sincerely grateful. He made me realize I had no intention of settling, and being in a vulnerable place had not shifted the way I upheld my values. Yes, I wanted more. And yes, I was perplexed by why he was so adamant about dating other people—something he admitted he wasn't even pursuing. But I knew I would be okay whether he ever came around or not. And although I truly wished he would, I wasn't planning on waiting.

A short time later, I was on my way to Los Angeles in the pouring rain to spend the weekend at a Tony Robbins seminar. Simply anticipating spending time with this master of destiny gave me hope and strength. So when my phone rang and it was Pierre, it was with that attitude that I answered and abruptly turned down his invitation to Starbucks.

"I'm on my way to LA," I told him.

"You're coming right by here," he contested. "Please just stop for a minute."

As much as I didn't want to make a detour in the rain, it didn't take much to talk me into it. If I could embark on a productive self-development weekend, I could handle seeing Pierre, I rationalized.

I dashed into the coffee house and collapsed my umbrella. Shaking the water from it, I saw Pierre wave from his table, looking like his usual happy self. But as I walked toward him, I could see he had an air of defeat about him.

I sat across from him, where he had a black coffee waiting for me. I took his thoughtfulness as a sign that I was still on his map.

"You know, Mary," he said, "you're so much more grounded than I am. You really know what you want and have so much confidence in pursuing it. I find myself feeling like something's wrong with me. What do you think is going on here?"

I was quiet for a moment, and then the answer was clear as day. "I think you need to grow up." I said it with no judgment or emotion. "Just grow up, Pierre. You're not a young, free-spirited, single doctor anymore . . . maybe you're resisting being the fifty-two-year-old man you are now."

He flinched only slightly. I can still see his face with the awkward smile and the deep desire to figure it all out, the foggy windows framing how beautiful he was in my eyes.

"You think that's what it is?" He seemed to consider it thoughtfully. "Maybe that is it. I guess it could make sense."

I didn't want to sound insensitive, but he'd pulled at my heart again, and I didn't want to play games. Gently, I said, "Maybe you'll take some time to consider it."

I got up to leave, knowing I'd better exit quickly or I'd be preoccupied with Pierre all weekend.

"Thank you for the coffee," I said, then disappeared into rain.

❧

THE NEXT DAY, Saturday, I received a text from Pierre telling me he'd made a date for us to meet one of the surgeons and his wife for dinner the following weekend. I stared at my phone. *What does this mean?* I wondered. I couldn't help but ponder if this was his way of telling me he'd thought about what I'd said and had taken it to heart. He didn't say that directly, though, so I was left to read between the lines.

On Sunday night, after I returned from the seminar, Pierre called and asked me to come over. To be honest, our relationship—if you could call it that—had ceased being fun and instead felt like a constant push and pull. Though I went out on the occasional date, it seldom resulted in a second one. Each man was kind and could have been a possibility had my heart been there. But it wasn't. Although Pierre and I had never gotten to the point of being exclusive, I knew I needed to disconnect from him if I was going to have something to give someone else—but I didn't want to pull completely away, not quite yet. Still, I was reluctant when Pierre's invitation turned into a plea.

"We've talked about everything already," I said. "I really don't think there's anything left to say unless you've had a total change of heart."

Silence.

Finally, he said, "Just come over. Please."

We did have plans for that weekend with the other couple, which told me he hadn't given up on the idea of us. I didn't want to get my hopes up, but I was curious, so I agreed to come over.

When I arrived later that evening, he led me to the couch. Almost shyly, and without much eye contact, he said, "I'm willing to try it your way. I have no motivation to meet anyone. I want to be with you. I'd like to give the possibility of us a try rather than lose you."

I loved that he wanted to be with me, and I was touched by his willingness to bend. But my strength was hard won, and no matter how much I liked him, there were things that were important to me, things *I* wasn't willing to bend on.

To test the waters, I asked genuinely, "What would your proposal of being in a relationship look like?"

I don't remember precisely what he said, but I do recall him saying all the right things to convince me.

"And our children will always come first," I added.

"Of course."

I took his hand and looked into his eyes. "I understand what you're giving up."

A smile spread across his face. "Yes, but I'm receiving a lot too."

It was getting late, and I was tired from my long weekend and all the driving. I knew he wasn't expecting me to stay over —it was too soon for that. So I let go of his hand and stood up.

"You know what the best part of this new arrangement is?" I said.

"What's that?"

"If next week comes and we don't like this, we can always change it. There's freedom here." His face brightened. "I'm really happy to be beginning this chapter with you."

He kissed me. "I am too."

IN THE MONTHS to come, Pierre and I shared honest and open communication about everything. If I needed to talk about Patrick or Bruce, he listened and was compassionate. If something was uncomfortable or bothering one of us, we discussed it. Mostly, though, we relished our time together and how naturally we seemed to fit together; Pierre's reluctance to commit had been replaced with sincere dedication to me, and I felt the same toward him. Only once did he mention that he was thinking about the life he had given up when he'd had a second chance at being single. My response was guarded, but at the same time I encouraged him to change his mind if that was what he wanted, that I could and would handle it.

"I don't want to change anything," he said sincerely. "That other life will cross my mind maybe forever. The same forever I'll happily be spending with you."

Some time later, for my own peace of mind, I asked Pierre if he continued to entertain thoughts of being single.

"Nope," he said with certainty. "I haven't in so long, I barely remember what those thoughts were like."

THE SECOND YEAR in my new condo, I received an offer I couldn't refuse. I lived near the Del Mar Racetrack, and people flocked to the area during the racing season. Someone asked me if I might be willing to rent my place out for a three-month period when attendance was high at the track. Right away I saw it as a great way to supplement my nursing income, and when I pitched the idea to Pierre, he saw it as the perfect opportunity for me to move into his newly rented apartment in Carmel Valley. He had recently rented out his big house, and he and Elan were now happily ensconced in a space more suited to two people—but that had room for one more.

"I'll be happy to share rent with my income from the rental," I told him.

"Keep your money," he said, scooping me into a hug.

I knew this was going to be a big test of our relationship. Between living and working together, we would practically be in each other's space 24/7—and Pierre wasn't the only factor. I would also be a constant presence in his teenage son's life. From raising my own boys, I knew what that prospect held. But I had never been in a role like this before, and I knew carried its own potential challenges. So far, Elan and I had gotten along well; he was a happy, curious, entertaining child full of enthusiasm for life. I was determined to return Pierre's generosity by giving my time and effort to making a lovely home environment for the man I loved and his son. I briefly wondered if I felt I had another chance to raise a son after losing Patrick, but that thought was quickly eclipsed. No one could ever be a replacement for Patrick, not even in theory, and Elan had a mother, so I wanted to tread lightly and not be too imposing.

After I moved in, I immediately began doing all the things I'd done for so many years for my own family: cooking breakfast and dinner, grocery shopping, carpooling, doing laundry, dropping off forgotten school lunches. I had always loved the role I had in our family of five, and I felt my nurturing nature had found a home once again—albeit a different sort of home— and it was a pleasure for me to take care of this wonderful twosome. I easily plugged myself into their lives, and with each passing day I marveled at the comfort of being with Pierre most every hour of the day and night.

By 2014, we were still maintaining our living arrangement—with me back and forth between the condo and Pierre's apartment, depending on the racing season—and the renters of Pierre's house in Carmel Valley decided they were ready to move on. Pierre was prepared to sell his dream home, but the one catch was that to avoid capital gains on the large profit, he would have to live two of the last five years in the house.

"It looks like Elan and I are going back to the old neighborhood," he announced.

Elan was a senior and thrilled to live in their large, beautiful home, complete with a pool, Jacuzzi, magnificent yard, game room, and plenty of space for friends. Pierre was equally eager to experience life again in the home he loved and had fought hard to keep.

Pierre assumed I'd move in with them—and he was clearly surprised by my response to his assumption.

"Well," I said, "I have my own home . . . and we do well being together most of the time at your house when Elan's home . . . and at my place otherwise."

"But we both really want you to come," Pierre pleaded.

But it wasn't such an easy decision for me. I knew that moving into his huge family home would feel more definite, and oddly enough, I wasn't sure about that final of a step. My feelings supported it but something in my heart made me pause. I needed to contemplate my reticence before agreeing to change my life again for good. We were clearly committed in a way that supported forever, but among other things there was a child involved, and I didn't want to be rash. I also knew this was my chance to have a completely different relationship from the one I had with Bruce. By then, it was clear to me that I did, but it was putting action to my thoughts—and pledging to share my life with Pierre—that made me want to be certain. If and when I took that step, I knew I would never leave.

One day, when it was just Elan and me at the apartment, he asked me for what seemed the millionth time if I was moving to Duck Pond Lane.

"It's going to be so cool," he beamed excitedly. Up until then, I'd been vague each time he asked, but on this day he pressed. "Mary, you *should* come and live with us there."

On hearing those words, something fell into place. I hadn't known I needed Elan's approval so directly. Or perhaps it wasn't his approval as much as a missing piece I didn't realize the puzzle was lacking for a complete picture. To be honest, I'd wondered if making what I believed would be such a final move with Pierre was a bit stalled because it didn't support my mother's value system. But with her recent passing, I couldn't help but chuckle; she was the queen of not seeing what she didn't want to see. Besides, at nearly sixty years old, I couldn't imagine her opinion stopping me. Yes, certain family values were hard to shake, but a lot of time had passed since she had adopted those values. I was not a disempowered person following antiquated rules; instead, I was making a decision from an empowered position of what I wanted and what I judged to be appropriate for my life at that time. I found all kinds of ways to honor my mother, but this certainly didn't need to be one of them. Plus, I'd been living for short stints with Pierre and Elan for the past two years. What real difference did it make that it was a house and not an apartment?

That evening, I told Pierre that after giving it a lot of thought, I'd decided to move in with them. He showed his elation by wrapping me in a huge hug. When he released me, he looked into my eyes with genuine happiness.

With a sparkle in my tone, I asked, "Can we make the house a home?"

We both knew that while the house was beautiful, it needed some updating, major repairs, and eventual staging for the marketing that would come in two years. The yard had suffered and needed attention too. Even though it was temporary,

I wanted the house to truly feel like our home, plus the improvements would increase the market value.

"Yes," he said sincerely. "We'll make it a fun project."

And a project it was, inside and out. The changes were gradual but the progress was constant. We moved things, painted things, added things, built things, planted things—until one day it seemed everything on our list had been completed. We stood together and looked around, taking it all in.

"Wow," I said. "We did it."

Pierre smiled. "We sure did. Now it really *is* home."

A LITTLE OVER two years later, in 2017, it was time to put the house on the market. We had made beautiful memories there, and our relationship had only become stronger. Though it was difficult to think of letting the house go, Pierre had hoped it would prove to be a good investment property, so we moved forward in putting it on the market.

Pierre and I were also both turning sixty later that year. I thought it was a great opportunity to celebrate with a big party—not only for our milestone birthdays, but also for yet another new chapter. I'd started life-coaching school the preceding summer, and I'd be graduating in June. It was a dream come true for me—especially as I began this new decade of my life—to be in a position of helping people identify what they wanted, clear what might be in the way, and guide them in figuring out how to obtain it. But even more than that, I wanted to celebrate *us*. After seven years of building our relationship, Pierre and I were both ready to plan a day that put the focus officially on our partnership and on our love and commitment to each other.

On the 4th of July, one hundred and fifty people gathered in our self-professed Garden of Eden. Keeping things casual, I wore a knee-length white dress I'd bought that spring on a trip to Madrid, and Pierre donned a white shirt, jeans, and flip flops. Standing next to the vanishing-edge pool, in front of our sons, close family members, and a myriad of friends who were like family, we spoke our intentions to each other in a simple yet heartfelt commitment ceremony.

After thanking everyone for being there, I turned to David and Matt. "You're the beat of my heart, and together you've been my rock. Thank you for trusting me, accepting my decision, and always being unconditional in your love for me." I'd thought long and hard about how to include Patrick, but I knew I couldn't do that without breaking down; once those tears began, they wouldn't stop. So, not wanting sadness to have a place in our day, I chose to be content knowing there wasn't a person there who didn't feel Patrick with us in spirit—and that he had guided my heart to leaving his name unspoken.

When it came to exchanging our vows, we decided not to follow tradition. Pierre related his through a story that highlighted my uniqueness, while I began by telling the crowd it was no secret that my family had seen its share of dark clouds in the recent past—but that those clouds had a silver lining in the form of Pierre. Then I teased, "I worked with Pierre for a number of years before he suddenly became charming." The anesthesia group broke into laughter. "But seriously," I continued, turning to face Pierre. "I love how you make me laugh, your integrity, your understated self-confidence, your strong stand on things you believe in, how you embrace your faith and respect mine, your love and zest for travel and fun, your love of family. I know we're going to grow old together . . .

thank you for stepping into my good life and making it great."

The guests erupted into applause as we kissed, and then the party began. We hosted an all-American cookout with hamburgers and hot dogs, and Pierre and I danced to Dave Matthews' "You and Me." At sunset, we all moved up to the massive deck to watch fireworks applaud for us in the sky. The entire day was a veritable dream come true.

That night, we fell into bed with huge smiles we couldn't contain. My heart was happy, my mind was at peace, my love was sure. I couldn't ask for more.

As Pierre wrapped me in his arms, I whispered. "Thank you, God. Thank you for this incredible new chapter with this wonderful man."

today

mary

⚬◦⁑◦⚬

OR THE LAST DECADE, THE QUESTION I'VE BEEN asked most is some version of, "How have you gotten through it?"

I can't deny that losing nearly every worldly possession I had in the wildfire, then having to say goodbye to both my husband and son to suicide—one intentional, one not—hasn't come near breaking me. I also can't deny that while losing both my parents and my brother didn't carry quite the same impact as losing Bruce and Patrick, there's no doubt that all of them had something to teach me about how we deal with death.

Reflecting on these losses over the past twelve years, numerous things have become clearer to me than they were in the throes of the devastation—and each of these insights has shown me just how strong I am capable of being in this life. Some have come to me through prayer, meditation, and reading; others have come from journaling, attending seminars, and gathering the courage to be introspective. In many ways, enduring the chaos growing up within my family prepared me for the trauma that was to come. Yet, grief has such long, extending fingers into areas you can't imagine—showing up like a person you don't want in your presence, in tornadic ways, often against your will.

Perhaps, though I realize our experiences will carry their

differences, you will find a nugget of comfort in what I have uncovered for myself. Or perhaps simply knowing "if she can do it, I can do it" will help you cross whatever rocky trail you may be traveling right now—or may travel in the future.

WHEN THE FIRE chose our home as one of many to devour, it was undeniably devastating. Having to say goodbye to almost everything I owned, being forced to start over materially, and not being able to replace myriad objects I loved put me into a whole new world of having no choice but to accept the charity and kindness of others, the majority of which was thoughtful and showed the most caring side of humanity. The house itself I had seen as being a place to create roots for our boys, and to provide that space for as long as they needed it, not as a forever home for Bruce and me. Although I never would have willingly given it over to Mother Nature, when it burned, the boys were indeed grown, and the house had done exactly what we hoped: allowed us to create countless memories we would always treasure.

But yes, I still struggled.

It was turning to Harold Kushner's book, *When Bad Things Happen to Good People*, where he references the term "act of God" that I received one of my first glimmers of peace after the wildfire. Kushner suggests that God is not all powerful but instead God is good. In each example he argues that God does not cause suffering but also cannot prevent it, that God didn't orchestrate tragedy to punish or teach, but that the experience allows man the freedom of choice to experience life's terrible things as we do. In the summary text of the book, Doug Muder states the following:

Some suffering is caused by the workings of natural law. There is no moral judgment involved—natural law is blind, and God does not interfere with it. God does not intervene to save good people from earthquakes or disease, and does not send these misfortunes to punish the wicked. Kushner puts great value on the orderliness of the universe's natural law, and would not want God to routinely intervene for moral reasons.

This deeply resonated with me. Believing I hadn't been "chosen" for tragedy, so to speak, lent a certain balm to my soul. But I also understood that I *had* been tasked with learning how to deal with the loss. So, instead of allowing myself to feel forsaken or like a victim, Kushner's and Muder's words gave me strength to focus on how I could move forward, and how I could get to a point of being able to let go of the past.

But just as I was finding my footing in a new environment, my husband was losing his. With barely a start forging ahead with my newfound strength, the unthinkable happened. Losing my husband and then my son in a span of only eight weeks, the question became: If the universe is truly on our side, how can so much tragedy happen to one person in a short time and not feel in some way like a punishment or being forsaken?

Hoping to be of help, a doctor I knew at the hospital suggested I speak to a Christian counselor at a church I attended a few times. I agreed. The counselor told me, "The day you lost your husband and son, God cried right along with you."

There it was again: the notion that devastating events are not a tool to punish or teach, and that people make their own choices and choose their own paths. Irrespective of religion, when there is a desire or request for Divine knowledge, we receive, but when there is a closed heart and terrible things occur, God grieves as well. Again, I experienced the deep sense of knowing that to be true. I also saw clearly that God *is* the good in my world, and that choosing to trust that is my choice. When we as human beings don't make that choice, I believe we live in a world of discontent, pain, and suffering. I didn't then—and I don't now—need proof of that, but I also realize that faith alone doesn't always provide that level of understanding. I know it's different for everyone, but for me, it's the strong belief of being held in the space of unconditional love that strengthens my faith to face what comes to me day in and day out.

I had to draw from that faith after Bruce died, and admittedly, it wasn't easy. I had to grapple with reconciling how he had left us, and why he had left us. I had trouble eating for a long time and lost weight practically every day. The people around me grew understandably worried, and so I made a concerted effort to "nourish" myself, even though I had no appetite. I had always been a runner, and I took on long distances with a vigor that was new to me. The endorphins had always made me feel good, and I was desperate for that feeling during the many miles I'd lose myself to the process. But instead of feeling better, I suffered a stress fracture in my femur and tore the labrum in my hip, likely because my bones were fragile from being nutritionally depleted. Intellectually, I knew I needed to take better care of myself, but it was difficult when I felt desperate to make sure my sons were all right, even though I felt disconnected and helpless in doing so. This made me feel powerless, and I probably put more pressure on them than I should have to convince me they were okay and handling their grief.

But now, all these years later, my sons maintain that I did the best I could for them under the circumstances, and I take comfort in that. I have also found this to be the time I'm clearest about Bruce. Even though he admittedly robbed our family of the foundation we all counted on, I feel gentle in my analysis of him and don't linger over any harsh feelings. You may find that surprising, but it is amazingly freeing to not hold animosity toward my husband for leaving the way he did. For a long time, in various parts of our marriage, I believed Bruce left me out on purpose; I always had the sense that something was going on deep inside him, but I could never know what it was. Eventually, though, I realized that he simply didn't have the capacity to connect more deeply. This is why I could never hold a grudge against him—he truly loved me, but he only showed it in the way that he could. When he came to believe he could no longer function in the world, he intentionally took himself out of it. It took time, but at a certain point I realized that no matter what we do, we are never as powerful as the person we wish we could help. If their mind is made up with a conviction within them we can't reach, we're delusional to think we can alter that decision.

With Patrick, however, nothing about the finality of his death felt intentional. His need to feel what his dad had been feeling, yes. His wish to end his life when he looked so forward to his future, no. There were so many unanswered questions; the desire to have my son back almost drove me insane. Thank God for those around me who objected loudly whenever I would express my guilt for not being able to stop Bruce and Patrick from taking their lives, for the "if I'd only" statements that plagued me.

As for friendships, two friends abruptly stopped being in touch, and I didn't have room to wonder why. The truth was that I completely understood how the circumstances could be overwhelming. In time, I was grateful when one reached back out to me, pleading forgiveness for her distance. Other casual friends extended themselves to me in the guise of support, but it soon became apparent that they were merely curious. Once that curiosity was satisfied, I never heard from them again. And certain friendships didn't survive the way I expected they would. Yes, the majority of people filled me with love, compassion, and understanding, but a few simply didn't know how to stand by me—particularly when I met Pierre. Some friends were over the moon for me when I found love with Pierre and embraced him wholeheartedly, while others struggled a bit. In those cases, I asked for their trust in my instinct to know what was best for me, and the majority, in time, granted me that. One person, however, actually had no space in her heart for my falling in love with someone new. In time I realized she was reacting to her own pain of losing the foursome that she and her husband, and Bruce and I, had been. But it still hurt. Thankfully, I came to a place of feeling saddened yet blessed and grateful for the way we once shared wonderful times. I even discovered that my love for her was unconditional, despite her incapacity to be in our friendship the same way—and I still hold out hope that maybe one day we can have what we once shared.

Through all of these experiences, I recognized that if anyone was a source of suffering for me, then maybe it was time to set some boundaries and learn to not let others' reactions be so hurtful. Over time, my philosophy about everything became: "What am I going to do about it?" Though this has been challenging when I've been steeped in hurt and confusion at others' reactions toward me, I believed I had to find a way to move forward with dignity and grace.

Today, I am no longer haunted by the things I was a decade ago. For the most part, I have come to terms with the loss of our home and possessions. I still hurt, though, when I think of my mom asking about the beautiful scrapbook she gave me for my fiftieth birthday and my saying I rescued it, knowing I hadn't. When I finally did tell her, as I've shared, she couldn't hide her disappointment and sadness. Maybe she was thinking of the only newborn picture of me, or of the memorabilia she shared of her college years and her friends and family who are gone now. It pains me that I had to be the one to tell her it was left behind. Other than that, there isn't much to grieve about the house anymore—but I did have to come to grips with one thing.

Though I never returned with any frequency, I would go to our old property, which I still own, every three to four months to harvest Meyer lemons or blood oranges from our many trees. By the time I would pull into the long driveway that now leads to a vacant lot, I'd almost always have tears running down my face. One day I made a vow that I wouldn't allow myself to come up again until I promised to think only of the good times. It has been one of the best things I've done; since making that pact with myself, I'm now able to enjoy the fresh air and beautiful views in which we raised three little boys, entertained our friends, and spent quality visits with our parents and siblings.

With Bruce, to be honest, it was a long time before I felt a deep longing for him. I thought it might be because we spent a significant amount of time apart with his flying all over the world. But I also think the way he left made him a stranger to me, and the horror shut down normal grief for a long time. I do miss him more often now and, interestingly, remember almost solely the good times. I reflect on how clever he was in building things like furniture and an entire outdoor kitchen on his long stretches of days off, and I remember how I'd exhaustedly call him on my way home from work and ask him to kindle a fire in the living room so I could come home to a warm place to rest and eat dinner after a long day. I often thank him for setting our life up so well that the boys and I are able to benefit from his planning and investing. He was a good man and I'll never forget that about him.

Patrick, however, is a bit of a different story. The horror of suicide made it worse in the beginning, and I sometimes marvel that I survived losing him those first few years. I thought the pain would kill me in some seemingly unrelated health crisis, and it was years before I had a day when I didn't shed tears for him. If it hadn't been for living for David and Matthew and being their example of moving on, I don't know what would have happened to me. Time does dull some of the pain and horror and at some point turns to sadness; the tears I cry now allow me to release a lot of pent-up emotions. But I still feel like I'm missing a part of myself. It's hard not to wonder, when I see the beginnings of soft lines around David's thirty-seven-year-old eyes, or Matt's thinning hair, what Patrick would have looked like now. But I've also discovered a newfound strength in the memories, as if the emotional muscle has been strengthened, so that when these feelings come up, I'm able to take a deep breath and carry on—what I deem the glorious result of continuing to move forward without forgetting the child I love so much. My heart will never stop being broken, but I've grown accustomed to accepting Patrick being gone more now than I resist it. A common aftereffect of devastating loss is equating laughter and joy with not missing your loved one anymore, but I've finally come to a place where I can tell funny stories to people about the zany things Patrick would do just to make us laugh—and I laugh while telling them.

❧

THE GIFT OF years has also brought me to believe that every time tragedy happens, it opens the door for revision and reinvention in life. Initially, it was simple things. I left twenty years of country living behind for beach living—the sound of waves, kids playing at the park, and traffic replaced the sounds I loved so much of the wind through the hills, the hooting of the owls at dawn, and the bay of the coyotes at night. But I adored being at the beach and was filled with joy looking out my window at the waves every morning while smelling the salty air. I'd sit on my patio and watch the moms with their kids on the playground and revel in being a spectator of life. At times, the joy of being on the coast was tainted by missing the familiar life I'd left behind, and even though time rather quickly healed those longings, I still have pangs of nostalgia that can bring melancholy if I'm not careful.

During that time of adjusting to the coast, I also was reinventing my home. Scaling down from 3,800 square feet to 1,800, I was able to furnish my new condo in cutting-edge style—something I'd never done in my life. With the expert eye of my friend Karen Hermes, the final product surpassed my wildest dreams. Calling the shots financially for the first time, I began to enjoy and take pride in my judgment and decisions. Despite my grief, I relished discovering that it was easy to own my life as a single woman, and I embraced it passionately.

With the subsequent deaths, however, I reinvented myself mostly in terms of how I saw the world. I've said there were times I felt as though the losses would kill me. When this would happen, I would look for information through reading, prayer, self-improvement programs, and input from friends and family. Bruce's brother, John, in particular, offered support through compassionate phone conversations and books he mailed to me, both of which were integral parts of my healing. His steady acceptance, encouragement, and love reflected my self-worth that had been so badly damaged. This allowed me, slowly but surely, to reinvent my future.

The beginnings of this reinvention materialized in the first year after Bruce's and Patrick's deaths. During this time, a therapist in town was looking for stories of overcoming for a show Tony Robbins was airing in 2010. My therapist asked if we were interested in being interviewed. We agreed, were interviewed by NBC, and were selected. But the night before we were to begin filming, we were cancelled at the recommendation of the legal team. As compensation, we were given VIP tickets to Tony Robbins's seminars, which proved to be life changing for me. Tony assigned me a life coach, and for an hour a week for six years, and as needed to this day, Michael Nitti was my guiding light. Interestingly, we seldom talked about loss. He'd listen when Bruce, Patrick, the house, Michael, or my parents came up, but then he would lead me gently and lovingly back to the possibility of joy and living life with humor—even interjecting the startling but strangely re-energizing notion of "so what?" He was instrumental in building the strong foundation I called "the rest of my life."

IT'S TRUE THAT I've experienced more loss than some, and certainly less than others. Throughout my journey, I've learned that no one could possibly quantify what constitutes tragedy. I know, for example, that a person can grieve just as deeply for a beloved pet as for a relative or friend; someone can experience intense devastation over what's happening to our planet, the same way one feels overwhelming grief after a shooting or natural disaster. We lack some degree of humanity when we take it upon ourselves to judge whose experience is "worse," no matter the circumstance, forgetting that we are all connected to events, people, animals, and aspects of nature in different ways.

Over the past twelve years, I've gathered tremendous wisdom, thanks to numerous caring souls and deeply appreciated resources. But perhaps the phrase that stands out most is: "Don't stay in the fertile rut of victimhood." My mom used the term "fertile rut" to mean that you're in a rut, but it's not a bad place to be. However, when people who see themselves as victims settle into a fertile rut, they tend to receive consistent comfort from the world as long as they don't stop being a victim. In other words, the rut feeds their need for attention, which is typically having people feel sorry for them or want to help them somehow. While others may tire of someone's "victimhood," that person will nonetheless sometimes choose to live in the effect of their circumstance long term, even forever. I did that for a lot longer than I realized, simply because for a long time, I needed to take comfort where I could get it. The problem was, it didn't allow me the power I needed to start implementing a plan to make changes—to climb out of the rut and create joy, happiness, and forward vision for my life. Once I acknowledged this, I missed the attention and caring from others that my "victim" attitude attracted, but I knew that love and connection could come from my own joy too. It was quite a slow road in the beginning, but I gained momentum with each passing day that I was committed.

If I were to give any advice to someone in mourning, no matter the source of the grief, trauma, or loss, I would say to definitely acknowledge that you've experienced an adverse event. In the beginning, the care and attention you receive from having been a victim of that event can be exceptionally comforting. However, unless your reality progresses to a perspective that does not include your loss or tribulation, you will find yourself living the trauma over and over again, simply to get that warm feeling of comfort, becoming a language of sorts that you speak. But when you make the decision to leave victimhood and start taking back control of your life, it is empowering. Yes, it may be a lot of work, requiring determination to implement a new mindset and choices, but if I can do it, I truly believe that you can too.

I would also say that because grief is such a highly personal experience, one that carries myriad nuances depending on the relationship and circumstance of the loss, you should never attempt to deny your feelings. You must allow yourself to grieve. Holding in your emotions will only cause resistance and disease. When guilt seeps in and you're feeling too much or too little, be sure to give yourself a break and realize that grief not only has an identity of its own, it has two sides: sadness, which is sentimental and gentle; and trauma, which is abrupt and frightening. Both are typically present concurrently, but recognize that neither is actually part of you, and that both can dissipate with the appropriate time frame and perspective.

While I recognize that no one person can ever tell you how to grieve in your particular circumstance, and I know there's no blueprint for how to navigate those darkest of days, I do know that reading about how others have coped can be incredibly comforting. This is why I chose to introduce you, within their own vignettes, to each of the places and people who will forever occupy space in my heart—because without an understanding of what our relationships were, it's impossible to understand why the response to each loss was distinct. As anyone who has experienced loss knows—whether the loss of a loved one, a pet, a job, a marriage, a home, or something else dear—no two "deaths" are ever alike. We may draw on faith or some hard-won strength to cope or even find our way through, but grief is definitely a process that lacks a blueprint. It can bring up cherished memories, regrets, relief, resentments . . . sometimes all in one day. Anger and sadness can rise up like a double helix of contrasting emotions; laughter can feel irreverent. I can truthfully say that losing Bruce and Patrick, in particular, were both akin to experiencing an amputation. Life became awkward and felt surreal until I learned to adapt; no prosthesis for an amputee feels natural, just like no person could ever come close to filling my void. I lost a part of myself that I will always miss, but thankfully, over time, I no longer had to change the dressing of the wound or feel the constant pain.

People often told me that no one had ever been dealt a worse hand than I had. That might have been true for them intellectually, but again, who can quantify another's pain of loss when it's so subjective? For example, there were times I wondered why I wasn't tortured by losing my own mother. I was sad, yes, but it didn't seem like enough at times. I thought maybe there were limits on how much and how long we can experience grief. I now know that for comparison's sake, I believed her death was part of the cycle of life. Her season was over, and that is why it hurt less. I likewise didn't really grieve when my dad passed. The tears only came when I wrote his vignette. Perhaps it, too, felt like his season was over, and after he had been rendered a quadriplegic, his passing carried with it a feeling of relief for him as well, which made it less painful for me. Michael was a different level of grief altogether; with him, too, I felt some level of relief, knowing he was no longer suffering with addiction and had joined his beloved, Luc. But I also felt deep sadness that although he had been able to live an authentic life as a gay man for many years, he was never fully able to overcome the trauma of his childhood—of feeling "different," encountering prejudices, and having his lifestyle interpreted by certain people as being "abnormal."

Whatever the real reason is for you, don't judge yourself for how you experience grief, and don't be something you're not simply to look a certain way to the world. Soon after Bruce and Patrick died, my mom and I were sitting together and she couldn't talk. I was crying but she didn't shed a tear. It was an "Isn't life interesting?" moment that I've never forgotten. We both undoubtedly felt pain, but hers—perhaps because of her upbringing and self-imposed stoicism—remained inside while mine poured out.

So I would further say that by knowing who you are and taking what comes with forward vision, you will find your way through the pain. To do this, I suggest engaging in healthy activities that make you feel good, and nourishing yourself with good, positive people and self-care—hot baths, nutritious food, gentle exercise, time in nature, prayer, meditation—things that edify you, not that harm you or temporarily numb the pain artificially (such as alcohol, drugs, or taking extreme physical risks). You deserve to be taken care of while you are hurting, and although many of us haven't been raised to prioritize ourselves, it's vital that that loving care your soul needs begins with you. Remember that you've been injured and that it takes time to heal. How much time? There's no way to know because each person is unique. Sometimes you have to be rocked to the polar opposite side to find yourself again. When that occurs, in retrospect, you can often see the divinity in something that could only be pain at the time.

✿

WHERE AM I today? I am a sixty-one-year-old woman living at the beach in Southern California, with two exceptionally resilient grown sons, and a wonderful husband who, instead of looking to be my savior, has stood respectfully by my side, allowing me to grow on my own, giving me the love and support I need to see myself for who I am. During the decidedly tragic period in my life, I definitely lost sight of that. It's true that who you spend your time with influences how you see yourself and what choices you make. For a while, that lens was cloudy. But with Pierre, I've been able to see my gifts through his eyes—those beautiful eyes that say so much when he doesn't have the words.

Over these last twelve years, my thoughts of sad days have dimmed as they often do with time. It helps that the present is so fulfilling, and that I can't wait to put my arms around the lovely chapters that still await me, both as David's and Matthew's mother and as Pierre's life partner. With Pierre, in particular, I have been on a path of healing, not because of Pierre himself, but because my true self is reflected in how we are together. When the inevitable bumps have surfaced on our road, we have been each other's support and ally. No matter how unsettling a challenge may be, no matter how much compromise is required, our greatest gift to each other is to be able to work through it with love and respect—and that is truly a beautiful thing.

Years ago, my friend John had told me I was in a lucky position for a woman in my fifties. "You're financially free and can do whatever you want," he said. "You *can* be and *should* be selective. Take your time. You owe it to yourself and your family to be happy again."

I had. And I was.

The aging process can feel daunting if you allow it to. But when I think of sharing those times to come with Pierre, I feel a sense of calm. I used to pray that God would allow me to know joy again—the kind that comes from deep in my heart, the kind that provides strength and endless faith, the kind that makes me burst with gratitude for those I love and appreciation of the miracle each new little family member brings.

Pierre answered that prayer . . . and then some.

I also have a third career now: after nursing and being a stay-at-home mom, I went back to school in 2016 and am now working as a life coach. This vocation fills me with hope for what others can do in their lives with the right attitude, choices, mindset, and most of all, willingness.

Time and opening my heart to learning how to live without some things, while being grateful for the new things that have come my way, has become less of a challenge and more of a joy. I've learned so much since that horrible first event in a series of six about how "what happened" is very different from "my story." There was no hope in changing what happened, but there has been endless hope for the reward that my story is changeable if I am willing.

When I hear people use the phrase, "You've got it," I think I really do. Just because life will never be the same doesn't mean this one can't be the best; *I* have the power to make it that way. My family is loving. My friends are my treasures. I am giddy with happiness when I think of the life I share with Pierre. There continue to be times when the dark clouds roll back in, but I am not so thrown by them as I once was. I am grateful that I have faith in being alive, as well as the privilege to love so many and to revel in the daily joys of my new perspective, not only with David and Matt, but that also whole-heartedly include Pierre and his son, Elan.

When it comes to my sons, I could write volumes about how proud I am to be their mother, of how inspired I am to watch them as they grow past their tragedy and take on their lives with the dignity and finesse of those who have known pain and chosen to be happy instead. But when it comes to the often challenging emotional roads they have had to traverse, it is not my place to share what those journeys have looked like for them; it is their choice to open up to others—or not—not mine. So, out of respect for their space and privacy, I will say only this:

I'm overjoyed that my boys are strongly on their feet after everything they've been through. I used to wonder, as I witnessed them struggling to cope, if we would ever be able to have lightness in life again. I even, for a time—though I'm not sure why I felt this way—believed I had lost them. But now I see that I hadn't lost them at all, that we merely had to get to know each other again and who we were as a family of three under our new circumstances. For several years, I held the umbrella they lived under, but with time, they found their way out from under it. Now, with all three of us nourished by the light, I wholeheartedly look forward to their future accomplishments and to what they create in their personal lives. They deserved so much more than to have their worlds rocked by suicide, and they've had every reason to be injured for life. But instead they're finding their paths, continuing to become aligned with their gifts, which fills me with indescribable joy.

I've been told countless times that if I could get through the tragedies of my life and come out strong on the other end, other people who have endured profound heartache could find inspiration in my story. It took ten years to feel ready to open my heart and consider putting my story into book form, but I can honestly say that I was ready to be heard. I hope my hard-won insights, while not meant to be prescriptive or expected to apply to everyone, will prove to be some form of inspiration for you if you're struggling right now, or if life brings you down in the future.

As Viktor Frankl, the Austrian physicist, psychiatrist, and Holocaust survivor so poignantly said in his book, *Man's Search for Meaning*:

> Everything can be taken from a man but one thing: the last of the human freedoms—to choose one's attitude in any given set of circumstances, to choose one's own way.

In some ways, I'm still on the road of learning to live with the empty place in my world and in my heart, but I've made a conscious choice to do so. Yes, I have sometimes trudged uphill a few feet only to slide further than I had climbed. But then I gathered the strength to pull myself higher—and because of that, I have continued to gradually, miraculously, find my way.

photo
gallery

*Front Door,
19185 Via Cuesta,
Ramona, CA*

*Drive
up
and
front
gate*

Aerial view of our home and 9.3 acres

Post-fire, entryway to our home, 2007

Sifting through the ashes—Bruce, Matt, and me, 2007

LTJG Bruce Odgers in front of an S-3 jet
Coronado, CA, 1976

Bruce's and my wedding day,
San Diego, CA, 1979

Bruce and me in San Diego Bay, 1993

(from left) Matt, Bruce, me, Patrick, and David
Ramona, CA, 2002

Bruce and his brother, John Odgers

Our family of five, August 2003

*The whole family came for Bruce's last flight,
2005*

*Bruce's retirement
One last photo in the cockpit*

Lt. Gen. D. M. Twomey, USMC

Mom and Dad, Ramona, CA, 1995

*Dad
and
Patrick,
1996*

*Dad on the
subway in NYC,
1999*

Dad's birthday celebrated with grandkids

Mom and Dad's 50th anniversary with
David, Matt, and Patrick
March 5, 2005

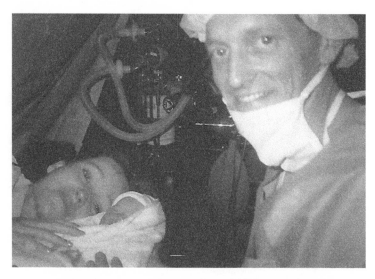

Patrick's birth, Medical City, Dallas, Texas, 1987

Spreading the great news, 1987

Our three boys on a visit to Ramona from Texas, 1988
Matt, David, and Patrick

Boogie boarding,
Moonlight Beach,
1990

A favorite
photo of
Patrick and me

Patrick,
1995

Cody
and
Patrick,
1995

David, Patrick, me, and Matt
Pisa, Italy, 1999

Patrick on the Ramona High Tennis Team, 2006

Ramona High Graduate, 2006

Patrick's visit home from Purdue, freshman year, 2005
Cody picked him up at the airport

Patrick and Danielle on prom night

Michael and Patrick, Plano, TX, 1988

Michael and the boys
Dallas, TX, 1989

Michael's birthday, 1989
(from left) Dad, Matt, Michael, me, and David

Bruce, Michael, and Luc, 2005

Mom welcoming Patrick Ryan
with David and Matthew, 1987

Mom's birthday with grandkids —
(from left) Eric, Matt, Mom, David, and Anne

Mom and me

Mom in Galway Bay, Ireland, 1999

Mom in San Diego, 2002

Mom and me, 2013, the year before she died
Wake Forest, North Carolina

Celebrating Pierre's birthday in the bush
Savuti, Chobi Game Reserve, Botswana, Africa, 2012

Pierre and me
Our Happy Day, July 4, 2017, San Diego, CA

Pierre and me in the Canadian Rockies, 2018

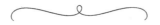

more

with

mary odgers

about the author

a conversation with
mary odgers

recommended reading

about the author

MARY TWOMEY ODGERS is a writer, registered nurse of twenty-five years, and life coach, whose default view of the world is through the lens of optimism. Born in the Washington DC area as the second of six children to a Marine Corps general and a former Navy nurse, Mary moved frequently, and by the age of twenty-one had had twenty different addresses. This nomad-like existence that required starting over numerous times, along with having to reinvent herself after experiencing multiple tragedies, has allowed her to specialize in navigating transitions with her coaching clients. In addition, she holds a Master Grief Coach certification.

Having made her permanent home in various parts of Southern California since 1989, Mary spends her free time hiking Mt. Woodson, enjoying walks along the beach, swimming in the ocean with friends, cooking, traveling the world, and relishing the company of her two grown sons, extended family, and loving friends. She also devotes one day a week to working as a post-anesthesia nurse.

Mary currently resides in Solana Beach with Pierre.

a conversation with mary odgers

1. **It's been twelve years since your first significant loss—that of your home in the wildfire. Why was now the time to write your story?**

   After Patrick's death, I was determined to survive my devastations of the previous year, and so many people said I should speak about them or write a book. I'd always loved writing and started documenting all my thoughts and steps I had taken to recover and to help my family recover. There's an intuitive feeling one gets that encourages the thoughts we carry to be put on paper, and after years of trying to overcome the pain, I knew in January of 2016 that the time had come to start the actual writing process.

2. **Instead of a memoir written in continuous chapters, you chose to tell each story in its own vignette. What was the reason for structuring your book this way?**

   Using vignettes instead of chapters was actually my editor's idea. She felt that this structure would allow each individual story to stand alone while at the same time tell my full story. We both agreed that the use of vignettes would give the reader a clear opportunity to see and feel how grief comes in many forms but is still grief. Each death shared the commonality of a forever loss, but each loss affected me differently. This approach was helpful in my understanding that it wasn't my degree of love or attachment to each person or thing as to how I grieved, it was more how I would, if ever, recover from the loss.

3. **Your faith is shown repeatedly throughout the book. Did your spirituality change through your losses? Was it strengthened or at times diminished?**

My spiritually has progressively grown stronger from the time I realized there was a God as a small child, when I was so willingly inspired by the beauty of it all, and has definitely grown through challenges. Before 2007, my faith was strengthened when my oldest son, David, was born. During the one hundred days he spent in the ICU, I had many opportunities to question if he would live or die. At four weeks old he had a bleeding episode in the ventricles of his brain that resulted in hydrocephalus. Infection could have wiped him out. My faith grew significantly stronger each time I thought he might not be with me for long, and I was determined to come to grips about what I believed about life after death. Years later, after the house burned down and we were left with such a huge void, I was committed to trusting God that we would recover and rebuild our home and possessions. Again, the relationship strengthened when I noticed my fears and sadness diminish as the path cleared to rebuilding a home. But perhaps the defining moment of my faith was the night in 2008 when the policewoman broke the news that Bruce had hung himself in the hotel room in Hemet. The horror of those moments were surreal, but I remember an immediate default into "what now"? The words that kept screaming through my head were, "Oh God, what are we going to do?" I didn't say

"Oh, God" like you might say "Oh, gosh." It was as if He was right there with me, as if *we* were in it together. I could have asked the policewoman—or Matthew, who stood on the steps sharing my horror—but instead I automatically turned to my faith. In the days and years that followed, even during the most despairing moments of loss, I never felt alone. I consider myself lucky for being open to that gift.

4. **It's normal for a person to suffer feelings of guilt and self-blame after losing a loved one to suicide. How were you able to deal with those feelings?**

It was awful at first. Interestingly enough, I felt much more guilt with Bruce than I did with Patrick. Living with a depressed person is very difficult, and my impatience was something I just couldn't hide sometimes. I was supportive of his mental health and, especially in his last months, I spent a lot of time in conversation with him about ways to reframe his burdensome thoughts. It was just too late for any of it to be of any help. I know I was distant emotionally for the sake of self-preservation, and I was not easy on myself at all after he died. The therapist I was seeing was the same woman Bruce had seen before he died. She plainly and lovingly listened and finally said, "Mary, you are not that powerful. Living with a person who is so far gone to commit suicide was toxic. You suffered too." Those words opened the curtains and let a healing light shine in, and although I stumble back into guilt on occasion, her words are comforting. With Patrick there was a lot of thought and conversation around him going back to school after his father's death. When he decided to go, we both felt good about it and had a plan if he changed his mind. He'd refrained from alcohol during and after his dad was buried and was proud of himself. He also had an attentive girlfriend and a devoted roommate whose parents were close by. Patrick was deeply saddened by his dad's death but in no way exhibited any of the unrealistic thinking patterns Bruce had exhibited for months before. Something about his death didn't feel right, and that is when I began suspecting that his intentions were very different from his father's on the night he died.

5. **You've said that anger must come out, but that you must move forward after that. How did you accomplish that, particularly after the losses of your home, Bruce, and Patrick?**

    I was surprised at how little anger I had toward Bruce, even when it became apparent how poorly many people viewed him for being the example for Patrick. Patrick's confidential suicide note had said, "I cannot live another day without my dad," but not even that pushed me to anger. I shuddered at how horrible Bruce must have felt with his hopelessness and depression and couldn't hold him responsible for Patrick in that state of mind. He simply wanted relief. But just the same, one of Bruce's tenets of a good parent was to "lead by example." How that single statement went from my admiration of his wisdom to his horribly self-fulfilling prophecy for our son. For many years, I accepted that there had been no significant anger, but I learned with grief that there isn't a true timeline. It was well into my relationship with Pierre that anger appeared. It wasn't like anything I'd previously experienced, and it wasn't always appropriate for the situation. It came on quickly and there was no stopping it, but it was also over as quickly as it began. Pierre was not easily drawn into it, but I knew that couldn't last forever. I'd always been feisty and spirited but this was different; this anger was clearly based in fear. Most often I wasn't sure of what exactly I feared. An example of it was when I'd wake up in the morning and Pierre would be in the living room watching TV. Was it the experience of the unexpected loss of Bruce and Patrick that I was tying to Pierre's leaving the room while I slept? I never understood it, but it was real and provoked anger. Those days were intense and scary, but thankfully, it passed as abruptly as it started. Pierre was the only person I ever vented the anger on. His loving reassurance when I'd regretfully apologize to him once the anger had passed was probably one of the most healing things that happened during that time. I was worth working through this challenge with him, and my confidence in being "loved in spite of" flourished.

6. **You say that "we take who we are to the grieving situation." Can you share the ways you've seen that play out?**

For me, I was always sensitive to others' behaviors and the effect those had on me. This was no different. My norm is to default into optimism about most things, and both my sensitivity and optimism existed during this time of loss. But what I also observed is that others respond to you based on who *they* are. This may seem obvious, but I discovered, for example, that someone who feels awkward expressing emotion may avoid you altogether when you're grieving because they have no idea what to say or how to be around an emotionally expressive person. This isn't a reflection of them being uncaring, but rather of a limitation in themselves. People's varying personalities and capacity for empathy, based on who you know them to be, definitely come through when you experience great loss.

7. **How did you allow people to comfort you? Did anyone offer comfort in an ideal way?**

Initially, I was carried by so much love and caring from family and friends that it was an indescribable feeling that gave me tremendous strength. For a full six months after Patrick died, I never missed receiving a card of encouragement in my mailbox—and that didn't include the visits and daily phone calls. It was this consistent outreach, of people assuring me they were thinking of me long after the losses, that truly buoyed me. Unfortunately, over time, I found myself shutting down and wanting to isolate from everyone except David and Matt. I needed deep connection with them and reassurance that they were coping, and it took maybe a year or two before I stopped canceling invitations I'd forced myself to accept, which was about fifty percent of the time. People were understanding for the most part, which I needed at the time, yet on occasion I'd worry who would be left when and if I was able to open myself up to the world again. Being back to work after a long leave allowed superficial interactions and the occasional coffee after work. People were incredibly loving and kind —I was overwhelmed with how their love and support slowly but surely began to heal me. But one of the most ideal "comforts" I received was from Bruce's youngest brother, John, who came right away after hearing the news that Bruce was gone. Since then he has been a constant presence of support and love for me and the boys. He, too, had to heal and we shared the process with each other offering prayers, books, memories, and unconditional love that I'm sure will go on forever. I've even dropped the brother-in-law title and lovingly call him my brother now.

8. **You say in the book that "we are only as strong as the people we're trying to help will allow us to be." How would you explain this in terms of suicide? In terms of other challenges?**

I had so many questions after Bruce died as to why he didn't let me help him, why he didn't let me in on the truth about what he was feeling or thinking. I have the reputation of being someone who will exhaust themselves to help a loved one or friend. For example, when Bruce voiced his concerns about having prostate cancer and what it would do to us financially, without skipping a beat, I told him not to worry—that I would go back to work full-time and provide health benefits and take care of him. When he didn't seem to feel better when I said that, I later realized that I further stole his power by saying, "Don't worry, I've got what you can't do." In the years after his death, I thought of all the things he could have asked me to do but never did, because he didn't want my help. It was then that I realized—with deep heartbreak—that when the suicidal mind is made up, nothing another person does seems to be able to make a difference. This is what I mean when I say that we ourselves can be strong in attempting to reach out or help, but if that help is truly unwanted, our "strength" in changing their perspective becomes diminished as the other person pushes us away.

9. **Can you expound on your statement: "Grief has such long extending fingers into areas you can't imagine."**

Around eight years after Patrick's death, I had a conflict with someone—completely unrelated to Patrick—and later found out that the person made a statement behind my back that I was probably the reason Patrick killed himself. I know that people sometimes say things flippantly in the moment, things they don't actually mean, but I was horrified and doubted myself as if it was yesterday that my son died. I had spent so much time trying to *not* take responsibility for things that weren't mine to take on, and in one simple statement, I found grief was to be mine forever, *if* I let it. I had to gather more energy in believing in myself than in the words of another person. I was actually amazed at how little time it took for me to find myself again, and for me to rise above the hurtful comment to a place where I believed with my whole heart that my influence in making my son kill himself held no truth. When I got my strength back, I saw the situation for what it was: another's suffering. I had to then ask myself if I could find compassion for them. I also had to ask if I could find compassion for myself and forgive. In doing this, I knew all my hard work to survive and be happy was paying off and that my truth was carrying me. When that particular incident would revisit me and threaten to bring me down, I would trust that God—not the world—whispers in my ear, reminding me that I had no blame or shame for what happened.

10. **Some say that everything that happens is guiding us toward a greater purpose or awakening our inner genius. How do you reconcile that in the face of tremendous loss? In what way has that been your experience?**

There is a life of greater purpose—and our inner genius awakens—anytime a person grows spiritually or intellectually. The saying about adverse life events, "If it doesn't kill you, it makes you stronger," may be true. But I have discovered that what works best is when your choices align with your mindset of living in the present and moving forward. For me, I do believe that because of what I've been through, I further have the capacity to help others, and I see that now as my greater purpose, however that may play out for me.

11. **How has finding love again changed you?**

I've had some profound realizations that I never would have had if I hadn't fallen in love with Pierre. For one, this is a new chapter but not a replacement for my old life. That was then, and this is beautifully now. There are things I wish I'd done differently in the past, and applying those principles to a brand new opportunity has been interesting and rewarding. There were the lingering thoughts like, "Maybe I was too focused on the kids," or "If only I could have been more patient," or a big one that took a little longer: "Why did I never see the fragile part of Bruce that had turned desperate?" These thoughts have made me more aware of my world and how each day counts. In the beginning, I told Pierre that every day, I would set an intention to be my best self in our relationship. There were always forms of that in my life before I met him, but I have such a different sense now of how life can change in an instant, and I want, for both our benefits, to be sure we understand the importance of living each day as if there's no guarantee of another. It's been nearly nine years, and I marvel at how I still can't wait to see him come home at night. I actually get excited about our evenings together. I know in part it's because it's just us with no distractions, but I do feel joy in my heart and in our life together. That is what I set my mind to when I was looking for another chance. I never thought I'd have to introduce my grown sons to someone I loved other than their father, but I burst with pride at the two of them, both taking things in stride for my sake as well as theirs, and for being mature and willing to see through what challenges we did have to a good ending.

12. **At the outset of writing this book, you had three primary objectives:**

    - **to show that life can go on and be beautiful**
    - **to show that there's no formula for grief**
    - **to show that evolution is possible through loss**

    Did any other wishes for your readers come to light in the writing of this book that you'd like to convey?

Looking back over the years since the fire, I'm reminded of my mother's words that there is a gift in everything. Even the worst pain of all, losing Patrick, had a gift. One of the boys the kids went to school with in Ramona called me after Patrick's funeral and said his troubled younger brother came to see his parents that week and divulged he'd been planning to commit suicide. It was the devastation he observed for David, Matt, and me at the funeral that he decided he wanted help instead. So yes, I do feel comfort when I have a realization that "if *that* hadn't happened, we would not have *this* now." No, it doesn't make it all okay, but I can at least be grateful that a good thing happened that came from tragedy.

I suppose I would further say that you take what you can get, meaning you grab onto the opportunities you're presented in each new day, no matter how small they may seem, to lift yourself up. I've come to see that although the human spirit can be fragile, I am reminded daily of how much strength there is in the boys and me. The only life my sons had ever known was destroyed, yet through pure perseverance we found our way back to being whole and complete as our family of three. I give them so much credit for that, and for their tremendous courage. At times, we had to "act it until we became it," but somehow, we did find the strength. It was on that new foundation that I found a man to share my life with —that gift of another chance at love that I know others find too. Not everyone may understand your openness to take your life in a new direction after profound loss (remarry, have another child, move away, go back to school, etc.), but you must never live your life according to what others expect; you must be true to yourself. In my case, I followed my heart with Pierre, and his patience and acceptance allowed us to pick up the pieces of a family that once was and create the one we have now. Our situation was fraught with opportunities for conflict; most people succumb to them and cause continued pain. But for us, we have all been able to trust and accept "what is." It is on that solid base that we've been able to build this new life, one I can honestly say I'm immensely grateful for, and one I'm hopeful my readers—if they, too, are on a path of healing—will find too.

recommended reading

There are numerous books that have given me solace and have helped me in my healing journey, and I share some of my favorites here in the hope that you may also take comfort from them.

Allen, James. *As a Man Thinketh.* Digireads.com Publishing, 2016.

Cowman, L.B.E., and Jim Reimann. *Streams in the Desert: 366 Daily Devotional Readings.* Michigan: Zondervan Pub. House., 1969.

De Mello, Anthony. *The Way to Love: The Last Meditations of Anthony De Mello.* New York: Doubleday, 1995.

Dyer, Wayne W. *Change Your Thoughts—Change Your Life: Living the Wisdom of the Tao.* California: Hay House, Inc., 2007.

——— *The Power of Intention: Learning How to Co-Create Your World Your Way.* California: Hay House, Inc., 2010.

Frankl, Viktor E. *A Man's Search for Meaning.* Massachusetts: Beacon Press, 2006.

Hay, Louise L. *Love Yourself, Heal Your Life Workbook.* California: Hay House, Inc., 1999.

———*You Can Heal Your Life.* California: Hay House, Inc., 2004.

Hicks, Esther and Jerry. *Ask and It Is Given: Learning to Manifest Your Desires.* California: Hay House, Inc., 2004.

Kushner, Harold. *Handling Life's Disappointments.* New York: Random House, Inc., 2006.

——*When Bad Things Happen to Good People.* New York: Random House, Inc., 1981.

Murphy, Joseph. *The Power of Your Subconscious.* New York: TarcherPerigee.

Prentiss, Chris. *Zen and the Art of Happiness.* California: Power Press, 2006.

Schucman, Helen, et al. *A Course in Miracles.* California: Foundation for Inner Peace, 1975.

Scovel Shinn, Florence. *The Wisdom of Florence Scovel Shinn: The Game of Life, the Power of the Spoken Word, Your Word Is Your Want, The Secret of Success.* New York: Simon & Schuster, 1989.

Tolle, Eckhart. *The Power of Now: A Guide to Spiritual Enlightenment.* New World Library, 2004.

acknowledgments

⚜

I am deeply grateful to my editor, Stacey Aaronson. Her insight, loving encouragement, and stalwart support have touched my life in ways I never expected when I mailed her my manuscript in 2018. Through her meticulous precision, judgment, and consciousness, she polished this rough stone to the sparkling diamond that this story is today. She was not only my editor and publishing partner, she was the healer of maladies and the love that reintroduced me to myself. I am forever grateful.

I extend my gratitude to all who contributed to this book by giving me the treasure of their friendship, kind words, and interest. Thank you to Lynda Niemeier, Valerie Lawrence, Maripat Lloyd, Ken, Kenny, and Cody Lloyd, Hal French, Steve and Jacki Neal, Linda Hall, Gershon Jaffe, Jan Ryan, Jeff Gan, Susan Keane, Shawna Allard, Ana Nieto, Billie Frances, Nancy Ruggles, Stephanie Donellan, Ruby Tovar, Cameron Kershek, Trish Anton, Paul Ecke, Bill Merrill, Noel Ecke, Karen Hermes, Jill Silverman, Sharon Saevitzon, John Lefferdink, and Cullen Bryant.

For Michael Nitti, Tony Robbins, Brian Conlon, Amy Hogan, Sarah Rangel, Michael Margolin, and Ken Foster, thank you for lovingly shining the light on my path to finding the answers for how I was going to live the rest of my life.

To Kat Schraeder and Jim George of RAA, you have supported me, educated me, been patient with me, taught me, encouraged me, and in large part helped me find not only my power in managing my financial life but also in believing in my capabilities for a part of myself that was new to me. My gratefulness is infinite.

I'd like to express my love and gratitude for the unwavering and loving support from my family, especially these past twelve years. We lost so much but I feel blessed when I see how much we've gained from our love and devotion to each other—Robert Thomas, Joyce Ward, David Twomey, Adam and Joseph Twomey, John and Jacqueline Odgers, Tracy and Fred Bareno, Paula Thomas, Sharon Nelson, Dan and Avis Thomas, Anne and Al Quinnones, Rachel and Graham Davis, Patti Carlucci, and Carol Clark.

To Pierre—you were and are the silver lining of what was once a black cloud. Thank you for always believing in me and loving me no matter what. I know that with you, anything is possible.

Finally, to my sons, David and Matthew. In the spirit of saving the best for last, I thank you for standing strong as we weathered the storms. Together, I knew we'd see the sun shine through again. You've been unconditional in your love for me. Thank you for your trust. Thank you for never missing a moment to show your support of me. Thank you for your loyalty and love. It was the strength that was still there in our family of three that has brought us so far. Together we are the solid foundation upon which we've built the rest of our lives. I am proud of you beyond anything words that can describe. You are my joy.

9 781734 093902